JOURNEY TO THE WEST

Journey to the West

A Play

MARY ZIMMERMAN

Foreword by Anthony C. Yu

NORTHWESTERN UNIVERSITY PRESS
EVANSTON, ILLINOIS

Northwestern University Press
www.nupress.northwestern.edu

Printed in the United States of America

10 9 8 7 6 5 4 3 2 1

Based on *The Journey to the West* by
Ch'eng Wu, translated from the Chinese
and edited by Anthony C. Yu (Chicago:
University of Chicago Press, 1977–83).

LIBRARY OF CONGRESS
CATALOGING-IN-PUBLICATION DATA

Zimmerman, Mary
  Journey to the west : a play / Mary
Zimmerman ; foreword by Anthony C.
Yu.
     p. cm.
  "Based on The Journey to the West by
Ch'eng Wu, translated from the Chinese
and edited by Anthony C. Yu (Chicago:
University of Chicago Press, 1977–83)."
  ISBN 978-0-8101-2092-1 (pbk. : alk.
paper)
  1. Wu, Cheng'en, ca. 1500–ca. 1582—
Adaptations. 2. Xuanzang, ca. 596–
664—Travel—Drama. 3. Buddhism—
Drama. I. Yu, Anthony C., 1938– II. Wu,
Cheng'en, ca. 1500–ca. 1582. Xi you ji.
III. Title.
PS3576.I66J68 2010
812'.6—dc22
                              2010051194

*To Anthony C. Yu, the most daring, diligent,
and beautiful of pilgrims*

CONTENTS

Anthony C. Yu

The story of *Journey to the West* (Chin. *Xiyouji*) was published in a more or less definitive hundred-chapter version in 1592 Ming China and almost instantaneously attained the status of a monumental classic of late-imperial Chinese fiction. Its skeletal plot was based on the famous pilgrimage of the priest Xuanzang (596?–664 C.E.), who traveled overland from Tang China to distant India in quest of additional Buddhist scriptures, the teachings of which were deemed canonical to his particular division of the faith. His furtive departure from his homeland in defiance of an explicit proscription against travel through the western frontiers at the time rendered him liable to criminal arrest and execution, but he fared much better on his return. The protracted and arduous journey lasting nearly seventeen years (627–44) gave him the scripts of his desire and also immediate imperial recognition and patronage. Installed by the emperor in the western Tang capital of Chang'an (the modern Xi'an), the pilgrim spent the remaining twenty years of his life as a master translator of classic Buddhist texts. Together with his collaborators recruited by the imperium throughout the empire, he gave to the Chinese people in their own language seventy-five volumes or 1,341 scrolls of Buddhist writings, surpassing the accomplishment of any scripture translator in Chinese history before or since. To this day, the sites (such as the Big Wild-Goose Pagoda and the Xuanzang Pagoda in Xi'an's suburb in which the priest was allegedly reburied soon after his death) and relics of his devoted labor as a cleric of the court can still be enjoyed by contemporary tourists of Xi'an.

Although the priest was by no means the only person who undertook such a lengthy peregrination for the cause of Buddhist devotion, the records and accounts of his experience (by himself and by his disciples after his death) in central Asia and in India made Xuanzang one of the most celebrated religious personalities in Chinese history. His own privations and sufferings during the journey, his religious activities during each stage thereof, his irrepressible spiritual commitment, and his stupendous scholastic achievements, no less the imperial favor bestowed, all combined to transform him into a cultural hero. The profile of this hero's story in popular imagination, however, quickly departed from known historical shape and events and took on characteristics all its own. Told repeatedly by mouth and writing over a period of almost a millennium and in various media—fragments, short poetic tales, short prose fiction, developed dramas, and longer works of prose fiction—the final version that appeared as the Ming novel had changed from the exploits of a human monk to a pilgrimage narrative fashioned as itinerant adventure, fantasy, humor, social and political satire, and serious allegory built on intricate religious syncretism. The crucial moment in this fictive transformation occurred when the priest took for a disciple a monkey figure, an animal guardian-attendant who was also endowed with enormous intelligence and magical powers. The pilgrimage circle was then enlarged to encompass Xuanzang and four disciples: the monkey, a half-human and half-pig comic (actually a Daoist god exiled from Heaven), a reformed cannibal (another Daoist pariah), and a dragon-horse as the priest's transportation. Eventually, the historical journey and the full-length novel diverge on this marked contrast: whereas the former is constituted by the determined efforts of a lone human devotee, the latter represents the combined exertion of a community of invented figures that, in turn, may be construed variously in the story—as different aspects of a single personality, as different constitutive elements of a process (an interior journey in quest of moral self-cultivation, spiritual enlightenment, or physical longevity through alchemy), or as different kinds of individuals in a society. The world of this community, moreover, spans the entire cosmos, natural and supernatural, generated by the multicultural religious imaginaire of premodern China.

My acquaintance with Mary Zimmerman, speaking somewhat personally, began in early 1995, when I was told that in about two months' time, Chicago's Goodman Theatre would be mounting a stage version of *Journey to the West* based on my translation of that Chinese novel, published in four volumes by the University of Chicago Press (1977–83). I was both elated and concerned, the latter feeling aroused by my puzzlement over how a late-imperial Chinese epic narrative (estimated to be about one and three-quarters the length of *War and Peace*) would fit on the modern stage. About a fortnight later, I finally had the chance to meet Ms. Zimmerman face-to-face for the first time, and, after more than an hour's conversation over coffee at Chicago's Bloomingdale's, I was persuaded already that mine was the good fortune—and even more so, that of this Chinese literary masterpiece—to have found so capable and brilliant a director as Mary Zimmerman to be the novel's first English stage adapter. More than anything else, the conversation assured me of the director's total immersion in the English text of the tale, mastering every detail of different episodes, recalling even incidental bits of characterization and speech, and observing unerringly subtleties of textual rhetoric and shifting modes of allegory. I remember saying to her as we parted: "You should come to teach my class for me! Your knowledge of this story surpasses that of many of the graduate students working with me on this novel at the University of Chicago."

Subsequent attendance of the play (I saw four performances) cemented my conviction that hers indeed was the highest artistic creativity. The translation of this late-Ming narrative onto a modern

American stage had been accomplished with the most daring imagination combined with the most faithful commitment to the original story's letter and spirit. The costume and setting capaciously sought to reproduce the dazzling colors and panoramic pageantry, while all the resources of the modern stage (trapdoors, side awnings, revolving platforms, audiovisual amplification, and the wizardry of lighting) were exploited at every turn to capture the three-level universe of Heaven, Earth, and Hell presumed in the narrative and to dramatize vividly the constant aerial movements, fantastic battles, and stunning feats of magic.

Like the Homeric *Odyssey* that Zimmerman had already successfully turned into drama, the Chinese tale is also one that fundamentally concerns the temporal traversal of space. To convey the drudgery of this drawn-out and hazardous act of scripture seeking, treadmill belts and sloping blocks made up much of the never-ending path trodden by the actor-pilgrims. To shorten the fictive fourteen-year trek into a manageable performance, the plot was judiciously and seamlessly compressed (sometimes with several episodes summarized or montaged onstage), while it retained at the same time a magnificent sense of beginning, development, progress, and climactic end. Throughout the play, Zimmerman liberally exploited a dramaturgical feat that has since become one of her signature techniques in several other productions (including the most recent one of *Silk* for Goodman): the presiding role of a participatory or nonparticipatory narrator onstage. This person's unobtrusive, informative voice both shows and tells the action, and, in this way, the traditional generic boundaries of drama and narrative are cannily breached. And, to help the audience hear the original story—at least in its English rendering—not only were large segments of dialogue directly scripted but also many prefatory or commentarial verses structured in the novelistic text were turned into haunting libretti-serving music originally composed for this performance. When the pilgrims neared the land of their faith in the story, the accompanying score became audibly more Indian in idiom and instrumentation. Like the Greek epics, the Chinese narrative is one that weds exciting entertainment to serious reflection. Ingeniously and consistently, Zimmerman's staging followed its narrative example and sought to merge rousing adventure and humor with Buddhist and Daoist wisdom. In this director's hand, there was never any room for cultural or audience condescension.

Since its publication in late-sixteenth-century China, *Journey to the West* has not only enjoyed vast readership among the Chinese people of all regions and social strata, but its popularity has continued to spread to other peoples and lands through increased translation and adaptation in different media—illustrated books, comics, plays, Peking and other regional operas, shadow puppet plays, radio show, film, TV series, rewriting (such as the work of Timothy Mo, Maxine Hong Kingston, and David Henry Hwang), and, reportedly, even a Western opera music drama in the making. Of its many features attractive to the old and the young, the elite and the demotic, one undeniable element pervasive of the story's invention is to be found in the multicultural character of the original no less in its fictional transformation. Just as the Chinese Xuanzang's efforts in seeking and translating Indian scriptures personified a lifelong act of cultural transmission and exchange, so the several worlds (sociopolitical, natural, textual, and religious) in which the fictive pilgrims played out their roles already revealed the thorough interpenetration of foreign cultures in early-medieval China and thereafter. The spirit of *Journey to the West*, whether in history or fiction, can thus never be monolithically and narrowly Han Chinese. Mary Zimmerman's adaptation of the story belongs crucially to the ongoing process of its contemporary globalization, but her script, for me, represents the happiest attempt at honoring distinctive cultural otherness in the universal medium of art. I hope that the publication of her play will inspire many to experience for themselves how exciting its performance can be.

PRODUCTION HISTORY

The world premiere of *Journey to the West* opened at the Goodman Theatre in Chicago on April 28, 1995.

Guanyin and others . . . . Jenny Bacon
Buddha and others . . . . Jane C. Cho
Musicians . . . . Sittisak Chanyawut,
William Schwarz, Miriam Sturm
Green Orchid and others . . . . Manao DeMuth
Jade Emperor, Tang Emperor,
and others . . . . Christopher Donahue
Monkey, Sun Wukong . . . . Doug Hara
Yama and others . . . . David Kersnar
Tripitaka Tang . . . . Bruce Norris
Moksa and others . . . . Maulik Pancholy
Pig, Zhu Bajie . . . . Steve Pickering
Sha Monk . . . . Paul Oakley Stovall
Dragon King and others . . . . Tim Rhoze
Subodhi and others . . . . Lisa Tejero
Woodsman Li and others . . . . Marc Vann
Fisherman Zhang and others . . . . Tracy Walsh

The set design was by Scott Bradley, costumes by Allison Reeds, and lighting design by T. J. Gerckens. Sound design was by Michael Bodeen, and original music was composed by William Schwarz, Miriam Sturm, and Michael Bodeen. The production stage manager was Barbara Burton, and Mary Zimmerman directed.

Journey to the West was subsequently produced at the Huntington Theatre in Boston and the Berkeley Repertory Theatre in 1996. Mary Zimmerman directed.

A NOTE ON THE SET DESIGN

What *Journey to the West* has to say about the nature of reality and illusion—and in particular about the flexibility of space and distance—suggests a wide variety of approaches for its design. It could be designed with great representational detail and period accuracy, or it could be played on a bare stage or in a white box. It could be architectural or painterly.

The set for the original production was a trick box of doors, trapdoors, and rolling stairs. Taking its cue from Monkey's line, "The whole of Heaven and Earth is one large room," it resembled the interior of a large, open, red-columned temple, from which the audience looked outward to a back wall of what appeared to be another building. This back wall contained two sets of doors: a smaller set high up in the wall and a lower set at ground level. The lower set of doors contained only a set of stairs that could roll out and retract in order for actors to climb to the higher doors as needed. The higher doors opened periodically to reveal very detailed, miniature, dioramalike settings in which small scenes could be played: a mountain peak with a tag on top, Guanyin's bamboo grove, or the Dragon King's tearoom. One setting, a replica of the full-stage set itself, was used for all of Buddha's entrances. Other times the upper doors opened to reveal the gigantic moving eyeball of Sha Monk or the cabinet of scrolls in the Western Heaven. For the final ascension into Heaven, the doors opened to utter emptiness, nothing but white light.

From an opening high up on the stage-right wall, a section of a heavenly bridge could extend and retract. From there the Jade Emperor held court, Guanyin observed the eighty-first ordeal, and the four pilgrims spotted the little boat far below at the final river at Thunderclap Mountain.

Most significantly, perhaps, there was a three-foot-wide slip stage crossing the width of the entire playing area, against the motion of which the pilgrims could walk without moving forward much in space. The slip stage was also used to allow the Daoist disciples to "drift off" to sleep and to bring various bits of scenery on and off, such as a thicket of brambles, a stool or two, a large boat with a lantern, or some small stair units of "mountains" for Tripitaka to climb over.

In spite of its seeming complexity, the original set had a rough, manual feel to it, and most effects were accomplished very simply. Flying was a "let's pretend" affair; rivers and streams were lengths of silk or little fans manipulated by company members. However it is designed, the play should move as swiftly as possible. All scenes should overlap one another with no blackouts.

For additional staging notes about specific scenes or moments, see the appendix (page 175).

JOURNEY TO THE WEST

CHARACTERS

THE PILGRIMS
Monkey King (Sun Wukong or
Pilgrim Sun)
Tripitaka, a monk
Pig (Zhu Wuneng or Bajie)
Sha Monk (Sha Wujing),
a river monster

IMMORTALS
Buddha
Jade Emperor, King of Heaven
Guanyin, a bodhisattva
Moksa, attendant in Heaven
Subodhi, a Daoist master
Death Girls, Yama's assistants
Dragon King
Dragon Queen
Yama, King of the Underworld
Peach Girls
Eight-and-Ten
Lonesome Rectitude
Cloud-Brushing Dean
Master Void-Surmounting
Apricot

OTHERS
Woodcutter
Tang Emperor, King of the
Eastern realm
Mr. Gao
Green Orchid, Mr. Gao's
daughter
Tripitaka's Mother
Tripitaka's Father
Grandmother
Boatman
Woodsman Li
Fisherman Zhang
Ferrywoman
Innkeeper
Daoist Guardian
Monk
King
Daoist Father-in-Law
Girl
Princess of Sravasti
Father King

Additional characters include extra Monkeys, Daoist Disciples, a Fiend, Attendants and Courtiers, Immortals, Officers, Robbers, Women of Western Liang, Demons, Villagers, and the Vajra Guardians.

ACT I

PROLOGUE

[*The curtain rises in silence. The* BUDDHA *sits in front of a scroll unrolled on the floor. He dips his brush in an ink pot. The* JADE EMPEROR, *King of Heaven, and the Bodhisattva* GUANYIN *enter. The* JADE EMPEROR *carries a lantern;* GUANYIN *is smoking a cigarette. They peer over the* BUDDHA's *shoulder. He begins to write. Music. The* JADE EMPEROR *reads the writing aloud.*]

JADE EMPEROR:
One hundred two thousand six hundred years ago, the Heaven and the Earth made love and everything was born.

GUANYIN:
Humans and beasts and birds all came into being, and the world was divided into four great continents.

JADE EMPEROR:
The East Continent and the West, the North Continent and the South.

3

GUANYIN:
This story is only concerned with the East Continent.

JADE EMPEROR:
Beyond the ocean there was a country called Aolai in the midst of which was the famous Flower-Fruit Mountain. On the top of the mountain was an immortal stone nourished for a long time by the seeds of Earth until,

[*The* BUDDHA *inhales.*]

quickened by divine inspiration,

[*The* BUDDHA *exhales across the manuscript.* MONKEY KING *enters and crouches down.*]

it gave birth to a stone egg. Exposed to the wind it was transformed into a stone monkey.

[MONKEY KING *stands up.*]

GUANYIN:
If you want to know how creation works through the spans of time, then you must know *The Chronicle of the Journey to the West.*

[*Music ends.* MOKSA *enters and addresses the triumvirate.*]

MOKSA:
Heavenly gods: Lady Bodhisattva Guanyin, Lord Tathagata Buddha, and Jade Emperor, King of Heaven, the light you saw just now emanating from Flower-Fruit Mountain came from a monkey made of

stone who hatched from an egg and has just now bowed to all four corners of the Earth.

[MONKEY KING *is bowing.*]

JADE EMPEROR:
Ah well, I'm not at all surprised. These creatures of the world below are made of the essence of both Heaven and Earth, and therefore, with them, anything might happen.

MONKEY'S STORY

[*Music. The* BUDDHA *and* MOKSA *depart. Flower-Fruit Mountain.* MONKEYS *are everywhere, playing and squabbling.*]

JADE EMPEROR:
That monkey in the mountain was able to walk, run, and leap about; he fed on grass and shrubs and drank from brooks and streams. He was so intelligent that soon he was made Monkey King.

[MONKEY KING *rises and separates himself from the others. He is crying.*]

FIRST MONKEY:
Dear Monkey King, whatever is the matter?

[*No answer.*]

What is disturbing our Handsome Monkey King? Why are you so sad?

MONKEY KING:

I must admit, I am a little troubled about my future.

FIRST MONKEY:

Oh?

MONKEY KING:

I have had a thought just now that one day I will grow old and die.

FIRST MONKEY:

Well . . . yes. But right now we have our blessed mountain and a feast every day and—

MONKEY KING:

But one day, old age and weakness will disclose the secret sovereignty of Yama, King of the Underworld.

FIRST MONKEY:

Well . . . perhaps . . . but . . .

MONKEY KING:

And if we die, shall we not have lived in vain, only to be born again and die again and never rank among the heavenly beings?

[*All the* MONKEYS *grow sad.*]

SECOND MONKEY:

Listen, if the Great King is so farsighted, it may well indicate the beginning of his religious inclination. Handsome King, do you know that there are three types of beings that are not subject to Yama?

MONKEY KING:
Do you know who they are?

SECOND MONKEY:
The Buddhas, the immortals, and then there are the holy sages—they last as long as Heaven and Earth!

MONKEY KING:
Do you know where they live?

THIRD MONKEY [*uncertain*]:
In the human world?

ALL MONKEYS [*variously, excited*]:
Yes, that's right, the human world . . . the human world!

THIRD MONKEY:
In caves and holy mountains and such!

ALL MONKEYS:
Yes, yes in caves! In caves and things!

MONKEY KING:
In that case, I shall leave here tomorrow and sail across the ocean. If I have to wander to the edge of Heaven and Earth, I will find these people and learn how to be young forever and escape the hands of death.

[*Pause.*]

FIRST MONKEY:
Won't that be difficult?

MONKEY KING:
Nevertheless, I'm going to do it. Now find me a vessel; tomorrow I set out.

JADE EMPEROR:
Dear Monkey! The next morning he got into his vessel all by himself and pushed off with all his might. He drifted out, out onto the great ocean.

[*Music.* MONKEY KING *sails on his little boat.* GUANYIN *walks beside him with a miniature version of the boat in the palm of her hand. She drops blue flakes like rain onto the little boat, and from above, larger blue flakes fall on the head of* MONKEY KING *as he sails. The voyage and the music end. Henceforth,* MONKEY KING *will be referred to simply as* MONKEY, *except when he is among the other* MONKEYS.]

MONKEY:
What's this? A human city?

[MONKEY *is surrounded by the hustle and bustle of humans in their city.*]

GUANYIN:
Our quest for fame and fortune, when will it end?
This tyranny of early rising and retiring late,
Riding on mules we long for a horse;
Already prime ministers, we seek to be kings.

[MONKEY *chases after various people, but no one pays him any attention.*]

MONKEY:
Excuse me . . . ? Can you tell me . . . ? Where are the . . . ?

JADE EMPEROR:
For nine years Monkey lived in human cities, and although he did learn to walk upright, he never found a single enlightened person.

MONKEY:
Nine years I've spent here, and I haven't found a teacher.

GUANYIN [*whispering*]:
Go out—

MONKEY:
I think I'll go out,

GUANYIN:
Into the country—

MONKEY:
Into the countryside.

[*All exit save the* JADE EMPEROR *and* MONKEY.]

JADE EMPEROR:
Monkey searched a long time until he came upon a tall and beautiful mountain with thick forests at its base. He went straight to the top to look around.

[*A* WOODCUTTER *enters with an enormous bundle of wood on his back, stooped over and singing to himself,* "Those I meet are all immortals, gracious followers of the Dao."]

MONKEY:

Reverend immortal! Your disciple raises his hands to you!

WOODCUTTER [*flustered*]:

Blasphemy! Blasphemy! I'm a foolish fellow with hardly enough clothes or food! How can you address me as immortal?

MONKEY:

Just now I heard you singing, "Those I meet are all immortals, gracious followers of the Dao." What can you be but immortal?

WOODCUTTER:

I can tell you this much: that tune was taught to me by an immortal, a neighbor of mine. He told me to recite the poem whenever I was troubled.

MONKEY:

You are the neighbor of an immortal? Why don't you follow him in the cultivation of the Dao? Don't you want to know the secret formula for eternal youth?

WOODCUTTER:

Listen, when I was young, my father died, and my mother remained a widow. I have neither brothers nor sisters, so there was no alternative but for me alone to support and care for her. Now that she is growing old, all the more I dare not leave her.

MONKEY:

You are a man full of filial piety, and you will certainly be rewarded in the future. But now, I hope you will tell me the way to the immortal's house.

WOODCUTTER:
Oh, it isn't far. Follow this path south for about seven or eight miles and you will come to his home.

MONKEY [*grabbing the* WOODCUTTER]:
Seven or eight miles? How can you be so close to eternal life and not go down this little path? Honored Brother, you must come with me. An immortal teacher is so close! Come with me, Honored Brother, we can live forever!

WOODCUTTER:
Didn't you hear what I said? I have a sick mother. Good luck to you, all the same.

[WOODCUTTER *exits singing. His singing blends with the chanting of the Daoist* DISCIPLES, *"Hail Laozi, Hail Zhuangzi, Hail Zhang Daoling." They enter led by* SUBODHI.]

MONKEY [*bowing to the ground*]:
Master! Master! I, your pupil, pay you my sincere homage!

SUBODHI:
Stop this kowtowing and tell me where you're from.

MONKEY:
I come from Flower-Fruit Mountain, in the country of Aolai.

SUBODHI:
Chase him out of here! He's a liar. Even with right conduct he couldn't get anywhere.

MONKEY:
What are you saying?

SUBODHI:
Flower-Fruit Mountain is two oceans and a continent away; you're lying when you say you came from there.

MONKEY:
Master, I have drifted across the oceans and trudged across a continent for ten years to find you!

SUBODHI:
So you have already traveled many stages? All right then, I will take you on. Now what kind of Daoist art do you wish to learn from me?

MONKEY:
I'll learn whatever has a smidgen of Daoist flavor.

SUBODHI:
How about the Practice of Magic Arts?

MONKEY:
What do they do?

SUBODHI:
You will learn the secrets of pursuing good and avoiding evil.

MONKEY:
Will it make me immortal?

SUBODHI:
Mnnn . . . no.

MONKEY:
Forget it!

SUBODHI:
How about the Way of Ways?

MONKEY:
How does that go?

SUBODHI:
It includes the Confucians, the Buddhists, the Daoists, and the physicians. They read scripture and recite prayers.

MONKEY:
Will I live forever?

SUBODHI:
Impossible!

MONKEY:
Who needs it! What else?

SUBODHI:
The Art of Quietude: fasting, abstinence, and the art of cross-legged sitting.

MONKEY:
Long life?

SUBODHI:
No.

MONKEY:
I don't want it! I won't learn any of these!

SUBODHI:
What a mischievous monkey! You won't learn this, and you won't learn that!

[SUBODHI *strikes* MONKEY *three times with his fan, folds his arms, and departs.* MONKEY *begins to laugh.*]

FIRST DISCIPLE:
You reckless ape! You are utterly without manners! The master was willing to teach you magic secrets, and all you did was argue! Now you've offended him and who knows when he'll come out again!

SECOND DISCIPLE:
Why are you laughing, you idiot ape?

[MONKEY *keeps laughing.*]

THIRD DISCIPLE:
Oh, never mind. It's getting dark; let's go to sleep and hope Master is in a better mood tomorrow.

JADE EMPEROR:
And with that, the little tired Daoists laid down their heavy mortal bones. And soon they drifted off.

[*Night. A bell rings three times.* MONKEY *approaches* SUBODHI, *who is deep in meditation.*]

SUBODHI:
You bad monkey! Why aren't you sleeping out front with the others?

MONKEY:
You know yourself, Master, that you gave me the order to come. When you hit me three times, it meant "come at the hour of the third watch," and when you folded your arms behind your back, it meant "and use the back door."

SUBODHI [*delighted*]:
Little Monkey, you are indeed the offspring of Heaven and Earth. I shall call you Sun Wukong: "awake to vacuity."

MONKEY:
Master, tell me, what is the secret of immortality?

SUBODHI:
Come close and listen.

[SUBODHI *whispers in* MONKEY's *ear. Music.*]

JADE EMPEROR:
He told him the way to fly through the clouds. He told him the secret to transform his body big or small. Listen, Sun Wukong, listen! He told him how to multiply himself into a hundred monkeys. Monkey, now Sun Wukong, listened to those words like jewels dropping from the master's mouth. His search was over.

[*A bell strikes seven times.*]

For ten years, Monkey practiced all the arts of seventy-two transformations. He could soar through the clouds and change himself into any shape at all. He became as agile, as active, as far reaching, as restless, and as brutal as the mind itself.

[*Music ends.* MONKEY *is showing off his tricks to the* DISCIPLES.]

FIRST DISCIPLE:
Do it again!

[MONKEY *flips.*]

SECOND DISCIPLE:
Where'd he go?

[MONKEY *flips again.*]

ALL DISCIPLES:
Wonderful! Wonderful!! How far did you go?

MONKEY:
Six thousand miles in a single instant!

THIRD DISCIPLE:
With skills like that you'll be able to work as a courier for the immortals!

MONKEY [*contemptuously*]:
A courier?

FIRST DISCIPLE:
Do more!

SECOND DISCIPLE:
Yes! Turn into a tree!

ALL DISCIPLES:
Yes, a tree!

[SUBODHI *enters.*]

SUBODHI [*angrily*]:
What is all this screaming and shouting about? Is this any way for
Daoist disciples to behave? Get out of here, all of you.

[*The* DISCIPLES *scatter.*]

So, Sun Wukong, you've been showing off, have you? Doing tricks?
You think this is why I have taught you all these years? To make
a spectacle of yourself for the unenlightened? Leave this place
immediately!

MONKEY:
But, Master, I owe you—

SUBODHI:
You owe me nothing. You have exceptional magic skills and long
life, but remember, you are not yet immortal. So don't get into any
trouble now, and don't involve me if you do. If you ever tell anyone
it was I who taught you, I'll skin you alive and break all your bones
and send you down to Yama!

[*Music.*]

JADE EMPEROR:

With that the patriarch dismissed our Monkey. His body was freed from its mortal weight. He had mastered the art of cloud soaring, and with a twist of his body he somersaulted across seas and continents. The trip, which had once taken him ten years, now took a single day.

[*Flower-Fruit Mountain.* MONKEYS *are everywhere, carrying sticks and such. Music ends.*]

MONKEY KING:

Little ones, I have returned!

MONKEYS:

Great King, you're back!

MONKEY KING:

Why is everything in disarray? Why are you armed? What's going on?

FIRST MONKEY:

A fiend, King, has been kidnapping our young ones and brutally abusing us. He seems to be made of iron! Nothing can stop him!

MONKEY KING [*smiling*]:
Oh really?

MONKEYS:

Here he comes! He's coming!

MONKEY KING:
Stand back! I'll protect you.

[*The other* MONKEYS *run off as a* FIEND *enters. A very brief battle ensues, and the* FIEND *goes down. Two women, the* DEATH GIRLS, *who work for* YAMA, *King of the Underworld, come in, glance at their warrant for the* FIEND, *then roll him into a black cloth and drag him off as* MONKEY KING *continues.*]

That takes care of that! But these mortal weapons are far too light. Where can I get something more to my liking?

GUANYIN [*entering and whispering*]:
Your neighbor—

MONKEY:
I know!

GUANYIN:
Under the ocean, the Dragon King—

MONKEY:
I think I should pay our neighbor a visit.

[GUANYIN *exits.*]

JADE EMPEROR:
And with one cloud-somersault Monkey flew off to the realm of the Dragon King.

MONKEY:
Neighbor! Hello, neighbor!

[*The* DRAGON KING *raises his head from his underground lair.*]

DRAGON KING:
Hello?

MONKEY:
I've never paid you a visit before, but now I am and I know you have all kinds of divine weapons, so will you give me one?

DRAGON KING:
Do I know you?

MONKEY:
I'm Sun Wukong from Flower-Fruit Mountain!

DRAGON KING:
Ah, yes.

[DRAGON KING *emerges, followed by the* DRAGON QUEEN *carrying a tea tray, two* ATTENDANTS, *and his own enormous tail.*]

I'd heard you had gone and studied the Dao and acquired great powers. You are immortal, I suppose?

MONKEY:
Practically. But now these mortal weapons are too light for me. Do you have anything you can spare?

DRAGON KING:
Won't you have some tea?

[MONKEY *snatches a cup from the* DRAGON QUEEN *and drinks in one gulp. Burps loudly.*]

MONKEY:
Thank you. Let's finish with the niceties. What do you have for me?

DRAGON KING:
Bring out the long-handled scimitar! This is a beautiful weapon, neighbor. I'm sure you'll be satisfied. And you'll go away.

[*The* ATTENDANTS, *struggling mightily, bring out the scimitar.* MONKEY *snatches it from their hands and tosses it about.*]

MONKEY:
Hmnnn. Much too light! And it doesn't suit my hand! Give me something else.

[*He tosses it to the first* ATTENDANT, *and it knocks him over.*]

DRAGON KING:
Well, then. Bring out the nine-pronged fork. A beautiful weapon, neighbor; made entirely of elephant tusks, rhinoceros—

[MONKEY *snatches it from the hands of a toiling second* ATTENDANT.]

MONKEY:
Oh no, this is much too light!

[*He balances it on his nose.*]

DRAGON KING:

Are you sure? Take another look—this fork weighs three thousand six hundred pounds.

MONKEY:

Too light! Surely you have something else!

[*He tosses it away.*]

DRAGON KING [*perturbed*]:
No, that's it. Let the high immortal take the trouble of going to visit another ocean.

DRAGON QUEEN:

But, darling, don't you remember? We have in our ocean treasury the golden-hooped iron rod that used to hold up the Milky Way. Lately, it has been glowing with an auspicious light: perhaps that means it was intended for our visitor.

MONKEY:

That sounds about right! Bring it up! Bring it up!

[MONKEY *scampers down into the* DRAGON KING'*s lair.*]

DRAGON KING:

We can't bring it up. It's too heavy. No one here can lift—

[MONKEY *returns, holding a teeny-tiny box.*]

MONKEY:

The only thing left down there was this.

DRAGON KING:
Open it.

[MONKEY *opens the box and lifts out a tiny rod, about three inches long.*]

There it is: the heaviest rod in the world!

[MONKEY *is puzzled.*]

Read the instructions.

MONKEY [*reading from a tiny paper*]:
Mnnn. Mm . . . all right then. Change!

[*He throws the rod on the ground. Cymbals crash. A full-size rod, three feet long, tipped with gold, springs up from the ground.*]

Very nice, very nice! This will do wonderfully.

JADE EMPEROR:
And with that, our insolent Monkey left without a word of thanks and headed back to Flower-Fruit Mountain.

DRAGON KING:
I'm going to file a complaint!

JADE EMPEROR:
Time went by like the snapping of fingers, and one day, feeling a bit weary after two or three years without sleeping, Monkey lay down to rest.

[JADE EMPEROR *exits. Music, a lullaby.* MONKEY *sleeps. The two* DEATH GIRLS *enter with their black cloth and warrant.*]

FIRST DEATH GIRL:
Yeah, this is the one.

SECOND DEATH GIRL:
Let's go.

[*They roll* MONKEY *up in the cloth and begin to drag him off. He wakes and struggles.*]

MONKEY:
What's going on? Where do you think you're taking me?

FIRST DEATH GIRL:
The region of darkness, where else?

MONKEY:
The region of darkness? Old Monkey? I don't think so! I have transcended the Three Regions and the Five Phases! I'm no longer under Yama's jurisdiction! How can he be so confused?

FIRST DEATH GIRL:
Not our department. You'll have to ask higher up.

SECOND DEATH GIRL:
Or rather—lower down!

[*They laugh uproariously.* MONKEY *scampers off to* YAMA. *He knocks on a door in the ground.*]

MONKEY:
Yama! King Yama, come up here!

[YAMA *appears. He is flustered. He holds an armload of scrolls. Many hands of the dead reach up to him and he slaps them away distractedly.*]

YAMA:
Hello?

MONKEY:
Are you the Emperor of Darkness?

YAMA:
Yes.

MONKEY:
Well, you're supposed to be an intelligent being. I'm Sun Wukong, and I have leapt clear of your jurisdiction. Why have you sent these officers to arrest me?

YAMA:
Relax. There are many people in this world with the same name and surname. The summoners may have made a mistake.

MONKEY:
Nonsense! Nonsense! The proverb says, "Magistrates err, clerks err, but the man with the warrant never errs!" Quick, get out your register of births and deaths and let me have a look.

YAMA:
All right!

[*He brings up the ledgers. The hands of the dead are grasping at them.*]

Let's see. Short-haired creatures, furry creatures, winged creatures, crawling creatures, and scaly creatures. I can't find you!

MONKEY:
Keep looking! Look at the file on monkeys!

YAMA:
Ah, here you are: "Soul Number 569 stroke 1350 stroke Q stroke 889 stroke stroke M: Heaven-born Stone Monkey. Age: 349 years. A good end."

MONKEY:
Hm. May I see that?

[*He grabs the scroll.*]

YAMA:
Certainly. I understand your need to verify—

[MONKEY *is ripping his record to shreds.* GUANYIN *enters.*]

MONKEY:
That's the end of the account! The end of the account! And I'll take the file of all the other monkeys too. Never bother me again!

[*He snatches another scroll and storms off.*]

GUANYIN:

And now you know why it is that monkeys live so long. For whenever Yama wants to come for one of them, the file is nowhere to be found.

YAMA:

I'm filing a complaint!

[*He crawls out and exits. Music.*]

GUANYIN:

We shall not elaborate here on Monkey's joyful return to his companions, for it is time now to turn to the Celestial Jade Emperor, Great Benevolent Sage of Heaven, who was holding court in the Treasure Hall of Divine Mists.

[*Heaven. Enter various* IMMORTALS, *including* SUBODHI, DRAGON KING *and* DRAGON QUEEN, *and* YAMA. *The* JADE EMPEROR *is hearing complaints. Music ends.*]

JADE EMPEROR:

What's this you say?

DRAGON KING:

It's true! That bogus immortal came uninvited to my ocean home, demanded a weapon of me, drank my tea, and departed without a word of thanks.

JADE EMPEROR:

Oh dear.

YAMA:

And he has caused enormous confusion in the Realm of Darkness. He tore up the record of names—so that inordinately long life is now given to the simians.

SUBODHI:

I believe I've heard of him. He is a mischievous monkey who has caused some trouble on Earth, but—

JADE EMPEROR:

Enough. This Monkey has caused trouble on Earth, as you say, and in the ocean and the Underworld. I sent for him already—when I heard there were complaints. He'll be here any minute and we'll just execute him.

GUANYIN:

Jade Emperor?

JADE EMPEROR [*not particularly happy to hear from her now*]: Lady Bodhisattva Guanyin. The Compassionate.

GUANYIN:

Jade Emperor, if this Monkey has skills as great as everyone says, and he has the divine golden-hooped rod, he may be very difficult to catch and to kill. Mightn't it be better, in the end of all, to be merciful, to welcome him to our heavenly court and give him some small position and rank?

JADE EMPEROR:

Hmnn. How dangerous is that golden-hooped rod, Dragon King?

DRAGON KING:
Very.

[*Pause.*]

JADE EMPEROR:
And his skills, they've grown very great?

SUBODHI:
So I've heard.

JADE EMPEROR:
All right then. We'll welcome him. But we can't possibly give him any real position. Just something to mollify him. Oh, shhh! Here he comes.

[MOKSA *and* MONKEY *enter.*]

MOKSA [*announcing as* MONKEY *has instructed him*]:
The Handsome Monkey King, Sun Wukong!

[MOKSA *exits.*]

MONKEY:
Greetings, heavenly court! These last two days I was thinking about taking a little trip to Heaven when your messenger showed up to invite me.

JADE EMPEROR:
Greetings, Sun Wukong. We've heard so much of your exploits.

MONKEY:
I judged that to be the case, and I suppose I am here for my official appointment. I've thought about what name I'd like, and I think I would prefer Great Sage Equal to Heaven.

[*Pause.*]

JADE EMPEROR:
Oh?

MONKEY:
What do you think?

JADE EMPEROR:
Noble Sun Wukong, I have an even loftier title and position for you, one that seems to be just exactly suited to you. That is, if you are up to handling the duties, for they are very important.

MONKEY:
I can do anything.

JADE EMPEROR:
Then I hereby bestow upon you the utmost glorious title of *Bimawen.*

[*The various* IMMORTALS *snigger behind their hands.*]

MONKEY:
Bimawen! That sounds wonderful! What are my duties?

JADE EMPEROR:
Oh, they are very important. You see those buildings over there?

MONKEY:
Yes.

JADE EMPEROR:
Yes, well, those are my royal stables.

[MOKSA *enters with a broom and pail.*]

Now, take these divine instruments and go there, and stay there, and be the companion to the divine horses.

MONKEY:
I am eternally grateful!

[MONKEY *takes the broom and pail. All exit except* GUANYIN *and* MONKEY. *Music, a sweet, light air.*]

GUANYIN:
Days—which in Heaven are like years on Earth—flew by, and Sun Wukong tended the horses with great pleasure. One day, he snuck into the peach orchard to feast on immortal peaches.

[*The three graceful* PEACH GIRLS *enter, moving in time to the music.*]

MONKEY:
Hello, young maidens.

PEACH GIRLS:
Oh, hello.

MONKEY:
What are you doing?

FIRST PEACH GIRL:

We're here to pick peaches for the Grand Festival of Immortal Peaches.

MONKEY:

Who is invited to the festival?

FIRST PEACH GIRL:

Let's see: the Buddha, the bodhisattvas, the holy monks,

SECOND PEACH GIRL:

the arhats of the Western Heaven,

FIRST PEACH GIRL:

Guanyin from the South Pole,

THIRD PEACH GIRL:

the Holy Emperor of Great Mercy of the East,

FIRST PEACH GIRL:

the immortals of Ten Continents and Three Islands,

SECOND PEACH GIRL:

the Dark Spirit of the North Pole,

THIRD PEACH GIRL:

and from the Lower Eight Caves, there is the Pope of Darkness and the terrestrial immortals.

FIRST PEACH GIRL:

The gods and devas, both great and small, of every palace and mansion, will be attending this happy Festival of Peaches.

[*Pause.*]

MONKEY:
Am I invited?

[*Music ends.*]

FIRST PEACH GIRL:
Ummm . . . we haven't heard your name mentioned.

MONKEY:
Really?

SECOND PEACH GIRL:
Well, what is your title?

MONKEY [*proudly*]:
Bimawen.

[*The* PEACH GIRLS *twitter.*]

Why? What sort of rank is this *Bimawen* of mine?

FIRST PEACH GIRL:
The rank and title are the same.

MONKEY:
But what ministerial grade is it?

FIRST PEACH GIRL [*twittering with her companions*]:
It doesn't have a grade!

MONKEY:
I suppose it must be the very highest.

FIRST PEACH GIRL:
Not at all. It can only be called "the unclassified."

MONKEY:
Excuse me?

FIRST PEACH GIRL:
Well, after all you're only a stable boy.

MONKEY:
Stable boy? Stable boy?

FIRST PEACH GIRL:
Yes, *Bimawen*—stable boy. We thought you knew—

MONKEY:
I'm a stable boy? I am the King of Flower-Fruit Mountain! I am the Great Sage Equal to Heaven! Come here, you bogus immortals!

[*The* PEACH GIRLS *flee as* MONKEY *takes his little rod out from behind his ear and throws it on the ground, yelling, "Change!" Havoc in Heaven ensues. Music. The* IMMORTALS *flood the stage. A terrible battle. Amid the havoc we see the Curtain-Raising Captain (*SHA MONK*) accidentally break a vase and another, the Marshal of the River of Heaven (*PIG*), make a pass at the* MOON'S MISTRESS, *who slaps him. This chaos continues until the entrance of* BUDDHA *in saffron robes and red gloves. All the* IMMORTALS *scatter, leaving* MONKEY *alone with* BUDDHA.]

[*Enraged, out of control*] Who are you that dares disturb my battle?

BUDDHA:
Audacious Monkey, I am Tathagata Buddha of the Ultimate Bliss. I have been hearing of all your audacious acts against Heaven, your wildness and your violence.

MONKEY:
Master, when you hear the wrongs against me, the injustices—

BUDDHA:
Injustices? A fellow like you is nothing but a little spirit, how can you speak of injustices?

MONKEY:
I know seventy-two transformations and a life that does not grow old! I know how to cloud-somersault, and one leap will take me a hundred and eight thousand miles!

BUDDHA:
Let me make a wager with you. If you have the ability to somersault clear of my right hand, you will be the winner and become the new King of Heaven. But if you cannot clear my hand, I will punish you and send you down to the region below to live as a monster a few more lives.

MONKEY:
You're certain your decision will stand?

BUDDHA:
I am certain.

[JADE EMPEROR *enters.*]

MONKEY:
All right then. [*Snickering*] What a fool. [*Aloud*] I'm off!

[MONKEY *somersaults and springs away. He arrives at a large red column.*]

JADE EMPEROR:
Monkey gave a great leap far into the air. When he landed there was nothing to be seen but two red columns and nothing beyond them. Monkey felt he must surely have reached the very end of the world.

MONKEY:
Ha! Well, just to prove that I was here, in case I need to negotiate with Tathagata Buddha . . .

JADE EMPEROR:
And that disrespectful Monkey signed his name on one of the columns and then urinated on the other.

MONKEY:
That ought to do it! I'll go back now and claim my new title as King of Heaven.

[*He flips and cartwheels home.*]

I'm back, Buddha. And now, the throne is mine!

[*He cackles loudly.*]

BUDDHA:
But Monkey, look.

[BUDDHA *holds up his red-gloved hand.*]

You have written on one of my fingers and urinated on the other.
[*Calling out*] Send him down to Earth! I'll put a mountain on him.

[*Two* ATTENDANTS *bring out a small mountain, grab* MONKEY, *and shove him underneath.*]

Stay there, Monkey, and think it over.

MONKEY:
Did this really happen? Did this really happen? Did this—?

[*The* ATTENDANTS *leave.* GUANYIN *enters and whispers to the mountain.*]

GUANYIN:
Don't worry, Sun Wukong. Be patient. Leave your Daoist tricks behind and study the way of Buddha. Until then, farewell.

[GUANYIN *exits.*]

JADE EMPEROR:
The brash, baneful monkey, symbol of the mind
May be brought to submission by Buddha alone.
He drinks melted copper to endure the seasons
And feeds on iron pellets to pass the time.

If you want to know how long Monkey stayed under the mountain, you must listen to the words of the song.

TIME PASSES

[*Music. Members of the company enter and sing.*]

Song
Five hundred years pass by like a flowing stream,
The work of a lifetime is only froth and foam.
Yesterday's face had the glow of peaches,
But today's temples are touched by flakes of snow.
As each dawn, the stars are swept away—
So even they, the stars, will one day be dust.
But good works in secret always lengthen life;
Virtue needs no pity; Heaven minds its own.

[*The song ends, and the company leaves.* BUDDHA *reenters.* GUANYIN *attends him.*]

BUDDHA:
Bodhisattva Guanyin, I have been watching the four great continents for five hundred years now, and the morality of three of them is acceptable; but in the East, it is not. The people there practice lechery and delight in evildoing. Now, I have here three rolls of scripture that could redeem them. I need you to go to the East and find a mortal, a virtuous believer, to come for these scriptures and take them back to the East so that the people there might be enlightened. But I warn you, on his pilgrimage this mortal will experience eighty-one ordeals as he passes through a thousand mountains and ten thousand waters.

GUANYIN:

Though your disciple is untalented, she is willing to go to the land of the East and find a scripture pilgrim.

BUDDHA:

Take your companion Moksa with you.

[MOKSA *enters with a basket, from which is hanging a little edge of scarlet cloth.*]

He has a scarlet cassock and an alms bowl for the pilgrim. If the pilgrim manages to reach the Western Heaven, he must wear the scarlet cassock so that I might know him.

GUANYIN:

Tathagata Buddha, the road to Heaven is almost impossible for an unenlightened mortal by himself. Perhaps he might have some disciples to accompany him on his way?

BUDDHA:

Whom do you have in mind?

GUANYIN:

Well . . . some old friends who lived in Heaven once but who were banished for one reason or another. This might be an opportunity for them to gain merit and find redemption.

BUDDHA:

Guanyin, your compassion is as wide as Heaven and Earth. I leave the matter to you.

[BUDDHA *exits. Music.* MOKSA *and* GUANYIN *begin to fly off. While flying, they talk.*]

MOKSA:
Lady Bodhisattva, we are flying rather rapidly, and rather high as well.

GUANYIN:
I know the way from Heaven.

MOKSA:
Of course, Lady Bodhisattva. But I wonder, from this height, will we be able to find a scripture pilgrim?

GUANYIN:
I already have someone in mind. I have heard that the eleventh reincarnation of Gold Cicada, a highly developed being, is now living as a young Buddhist monk in the court of the mortal ruler of the East, the Tang Emperor.

MOKSA:
How will you be certain he is the one?

GUANYIN:
Oh, we'll test him first.

MOKSA:
How?

GUANYIN:
We will transform ourselves and ask him a few questions. But we need to make a detour on the way. I have good news for a monkey under a mountain.

THE TANG COURT

[*The Tang court. The* TANG EMPEROR *sits on high surrounded by his* COURTIERS, OFFICERS, *and Buddhist* MONKS. *A monk who will become* TRIPITAKA *is among them. Several* COURTIERS *hold pine branches pointed straight up like little trees.*]

TANG EMPEROR:
If there are no more petitions, we will adjourn for today—

OFFICER:
Your humble officer begs pardon from the Lord Emperor Tang.

TANG EMPEROR:
What is it?

OFFICER:
There are two travelers outside—mendicant monks, my lord, who claim to come from the western territories. They say they are interested in questioning the most knowledgeable among our priests in order to compare their knowledge of scripture with ours.

TANG EMPEROR [*to* TRIPITAKA]:
My own holy monk, you are the most learned among us: Would you submit to such an exchange of Buddhist teaching?

TRIPITAKA:
Your humble servant would be delighted.

TANG EMPEROR:
Show them in. [*To* TRIPITAKA] Now stand by my side that all may hear your responses to these travelers. Surely, your knowledge of scripture will astound them.

[*The travelers,* GUANYIN *and* MOKSA, *disguised as aged monks, enter.*]

Here they are. You may proceed.

GUANYIN [*disguised*]:
So, Priest, you say you know the Buddhist scriptures?

TRIPITAKA:
Yes, I do.

GUANYIN:
May we compare our knowledge?

TRIPITAKA:
Of course.

GUANYIN:
Do you know the parable of the arrow?

TRIPITAKA:
A man is wounded by an arrow in battle. He wants to know the name of the archer, what rank he is, where he was standing when he shot, what the length of the arrow is, and what it is made of. As he is discussing these things, he dies. The Buddha teaches that one must pull the arrow out.

GUANYIN:
What is the arrow?

TRIPITAKA:
The universe.

GUANYIN:
Who is your greatest enemy?

TRIPITAKA:
My own thoughts.

GUANYIN:
What is the greatest crime?

TRIPITAKA:
Hatred.

GUANYIN:
The greatest sorrow?

TRIPITAKA:
Possessions.

GUANYIN:
How does one find happiness?

TRIPITAKA:
Act with a pure heart, and happiness will follow you like a shadow, unshakable.

GUANYIN:
And how does one find suffering?

TRIPITAKA:
By pursuing happiness.

GUANYIN:
Well done, Gold Cicada!

TANG EMPEROR:
Gold Cic—? What is he saying? Who is Gold Cic—?

TRIPITAKA:
That name!

TANG EMPEROR:
What is he saying?

TRIPITAKA:
How do you know—?

TANG EMPEROR:
Who is Gold Cicada?

GUANYIN:
How do I find truth?

TRIPITAKA:
You must cease to have opinions. But—

GUANYIN:
And Buddha has said, if you meet Buddha on the road, you must—

TANG EMPEROR:
Who is Gold Cicada?

TRIPITAKA [*to* GUANYIN]:
—you must kill him. But my childhood name—

44

GUANYIN:
Young priest, tell me, what is a bodhisattva?

TRIPITAKA:
A bodhisattva is one so enlightened he stands on the brink of Heaven and yet turns back. He cannot bear the thought of leaving others behind, and so remains on Earth to aid the unenlightened.

GUANYIN:
Tell me, do you suppose you could recognize a bodhisattva?

TRIPITAKA:
Could I—?

GUANYIN:
Yes, if one such lonely saint stood before you, would you know her?

TRIPITAKA:
Certainly. Yes.

GUANYIN:
I see. Emperor, this master of yours is answering only according to the teachings of the Little Vehicle, which, while full of wisdom, cannot lead the lost to Heaven. I have in my possession the Tripitaka, the Great Vehicle Law of Buddha, which is able to save the damned and fashion the indestructible body.

TRIPITAKA [*greatly excited*]:
You have this with you? Can you recite it now?

GUANYIN:
Why certainly . . .

[*Suddenly* GUANYIN *reveals herself and flies into the air. All of the court cowers and bows, including the* TANG EMPEROR. *All but* TRIPITAKA *chant, "Guanyin Pusa Bodhisattva" throughout* GUANYIN'S *visitation.*]

So, you think that you would know me, dear Gold Cicada? You saw nothing but that old shell, not the true spirit of Guanyin. Although you recite very well, you have not gained insight, Gold Cicada: you are still trusting to those old robbers, your eyes and your ears.

TRIPITAKA:
Forgive me, Lady Bodhisattva.

GUANYIN:
I have a message for the court from Tathagata Buddha:
We greet the great Ruler of Tang,
Mighty Emperor of the East.
Our Western Heaven lies
One hundred and eight thousand miles away;
There we have the sublime scriptures of the Great Vehicle,
Called the Tripitaka.
Send your most devout to seek these books
Over innumerable mountains and rivers and back.
If he is willing to go,
Let him take this scarlet cassock
To wear when he reaches the West
And this golden alms bowl to beg along the way.
If he succeeds, he'll become a Buddha of gold.

[GUANYIN *and* MOKSA *disappear, leaving the alms bowl and the basket containing the scarlet robe.*]

TANG EMPEROR:

The decree of the bodhisattva is clear. Young Monk, are you willing to seek these scriptures from the Buddha in the Western Heaven?

TRIPITAKA:

Though your poor monk has no talents, he is willing to go to the West on behalf of Your Majesty.

TANG EMPEROR:

If this is true, we are willing to become bond brothers with you, our brother, and Holy Monk.

TRIPITAKA:

But Your Majesty . . .

TANG EMPEROR:

Let the proper documents be drawn up: Holy Monk, what is your byname?

TRIPITAKA:

Your poor monk is a person who has left the family. He dares not assume a byname.

TANG EMPEROR:

The bodhisattva said earlier that the scriptures were called the Tripitaka. Our brother may take that as a byname.

[TRIPITAKA *bows.* GUANYIN *reenters, unnoticed, invisible.*]

We must consult the court astrologer for the auspicious day and hour on which to begin your journey.

GUANYIN:

All was done as ordered. And the most auspicious day was the very next one.

TANG EMPEROR:

Holy Monk, I have heard that the way to the West is filled with tigers, leopards, and all kinds of monsters. I fear there may be a departure but no return for you. Are you still resolved to make this journey?

TRIPITAKA:

I am. Although, it is true, of course, that I have no knowledge of how I shall fare or whether good or evil awaits me.

TANG EMPEROR [*handing him a scroll bound with a gold ribbon*]:
Then here is your travel rescript, stating that you are a scripture pilgrim seeking scriptures in the West and that you are to be given free passage. You must have it certified in every land through which you pass. And now, a toast.

TRIPITAKA:

Your Majesty, your poor monk has practiced abstinence since birth.

TANG EMPEROR:

Today's journey is not to be compared with any ordinary event. Please drink one cup of this vegetarian wine, and accept our good wishes with the toast.

[*He scoops up a bit of earth, puts it in* TRIPITAKA's *wine, and hands some to him.* TRIPITAKA *has no idea what the gesture means.*]

Dear Brother, how long will it take you to come back from the Western Heaven?

GUANYIN [*whispering*]:
After I leave . . .

TRIPITAKA:
After I leave . . .

GUANYIN:
wait for me sixteen years . . .

TRIPITAKA:
wait two or three years . . .

GUANYIN:
sixteen years . . .

TRIPITAKA:
or six or seven years at the most.

GUANYIN AND TRIPITAKA:
One day, you will see the branches of the pine trees within our gates all pointing eastward. Then you will know that I am about to return.

TRIPITAKA:
If not, I shall not be coming back.

TANG EMPEROR:
The years are long and the journey is great. Drink this, Royal Brother, and remember: treasure a handful of dirt from your home more than ten thousand pieces of foreign gold.

MEETING MONKEY

[*Music.* TRIPITAKA *departs with his staff and the basket containing the alms bowl and scarlet robe. The scene of the Tang court with its pine trees fades away.* TRIPITAKA *is full of determination and energy, but very soon he loses his way and is walking in circles. The music slows down, drags, and finally stops.* TRIPITAKA *sits down to cry.*]

TRIPITAKA:
This seems very difficult already. I've lost my way and I don't know where I am.

[*A little scroll drops from the sky.* TRIPITAKA *picks it up and reads.*]

This journey you have begun
How can you know the end?
You will be assisted by divine disciples;
But do not blame the scriptures
For all the hardship that you find.

MONKEY [*overhearing him, under the mountain*]:
Master, why have you taken so long to get here? Welcome! Welcome! Get me out, and I'll protect you on your way to the Western Heaven!

TRIPITAKA:
Hello? Who's there?

MONKEY:
Are you someone sent by the Tang Emperor of the East to go seek scriptures in the Western Heaven?

TRIPITAKA:
Why do you ask?

MONKEY:
The bodhisattva told me to expect you! She long ago converted me from Daoism to Buddhism. I am destined to be your disciple and protect you on your way to the Western Heaven. I've been waiting night and day!

TRIPITAKA:
Although you have this good intention, how can I free you? I have no ax or drill . . .

MONKEY:
At the very top of this mountain, there is a tag stamped with the Golden Letters of our Buddha Tathagata. Go up there and lift the tag.

TRIPITAKA:
Wait a minute. How do I know you are speaking the truth?

MONKEY:
It's the truth! I dare not lie!

[TRIPITAKA *heads up the mountain.*]

TRIPITAKA [*praying*]:
Buddha: If it is so ordained that this Monkey be my companion on the way to the Western Heaven, let me lift up this seal. If he is not predestined to be my disciple, if he is only a cruel monster trying to deceive me, let me not lift up this seal.

[*He lifts the seal. A great rumbling begins.*]

MONKEY:
Stand back! Cover your ears! I don't want to frighten you!

[*The Earth shakes.* MONKEY *lifts the mountain off himself and shouts in delight. He flips and scampers around. Finally he throws himself at* TRIPITAKA'*s feet.*]

Master, I am yours!

TRIPITAKA:
Oh, so you're a monkey.

MONKEY [*taking the basket from* TRIPITAKA]:
I will serve you to the best of my ability so that I may achieve merit in the eyes of Buddha and find redemption.

TRIPITAKA:
Disciple, what is your surname?

MONKEY:
My surname is Sun.

TRIPITAKA:
Let me give you a religious name so that it will be convenient to address you.

MONKEY:
This noble thought of the master is deeply appreciated, but I already have a religious name. I am called Sun Wukong: "awake to vacuity."

TRIPITAKA:

It exactly fits the emphasis of our denomination. But look at you, you look rather like a little acolyte. Let me give you a nickname and call you Pilgrim Sun. How's that?

MONKEY:

Good! Good! Now, Master, let's be on our way.

THE SIX ROBBERS

[*Music. The pilgrims travel.* JADE EMPEROR *enters.*]

JADE EMPEROR:

We were telling you about old Monkey and Tripitaka Tang, who were making their way across the first series of mountains on the westward journey. If you want to understand the true nature of this journey, you must listen carefully to the names of those they meet in this next scene.

[JADE EMPEROR *exits. Suddenly* MONKEY *and* TRIPITAKA *are accosted by six* ROBBERS. *Music ends.*]

FIRST ROBBER:

Stop, Monk! Drop your luggage, and empty your purse, and take off your clothes!

[TRIPITAKA *faints.* MONKEY *rushes to him.*]

MONKEY:

Don't be alarmed, Master. Just some people coming to give us clothes and a little travel allowance!

TRIPITAKA:

Pilgrim, you must be hard of hearing! They told us to *leave* our luggage and our clothes, and you want to ask them for a travel allowance?

MONKEY:

Just stay here, and let old Monkey take care of it.

TRIPITAKA:

There are six big fellows over there, and you are such a tiny person!

[MONKEY *sits down in front of the* ROBBERS.]

MONKEY:

Sirs, why are you blocking the path of this poor monk?

FIRST ROBBER:

We are kings of the highway—though you seem to be ignorant of it! Leave your belongings at once, and we'll let you live. But if you utter half a no, you'll be chopped to pieces!

MONKEY:

I have been a king myself for centuries, but I have yet to learn your illustrious names.

FIRST ROBBER:

So you really don't know? I am Mr. Eye that sees and delights.

SECOND ROBBER:

I am Mr. Ear.

THIRD ROBBER:

I am Mr. Nose.

FOURTH ROBBER:
I am Mr. Tongue that tastes and desires.

FIFTH ROBBER:
I am Mr. Mind that perceives and covets.

SIXTH ROBBER:
I am Mr. Body that bears and suffers.

MONKEY [*laughing*]:
You are nothing but six hairy brigands who have failed to recognize in me a person who has left the family, your proper master. How dare you bar my way? Bring out the treasures you have stolen so that we can divide them into seven portions.

FIRST ROBBER:
You reckless monk! You think we'll share our loot with you?

[*The six* ROBBERS *raise their sticks and try to hit* MONKEY *on the head three times, but the sticks stop in the air above* MONKEY's *head. They try again. And again.*]

SECOND ROBBER:
He really does have a hard head!

MONKEY:
Passably so! But your hands must be getting tired from all that exercise. It's about time for old Monkey to take out his rod for a little entertainment.

[*He takes his golden-hooped rod from behind his ear.*]

THIRD ROBBER:
This monk must be an acupuncture man in disguise.

FOURTH ROBBER:
We're not sick! Why bring out a little needle?

[MONKEY *throws his rod on the ground.*]

MONKEY:
Change!

[*A full-size rod springs up from the ground.* MONKEY *catches it.*]

Now, don't run off! Let old Monkey try his hand.

[*He kills a* ROBBER. *Then he kills all of them.*]

You may proceed now, Master. Those robbers have been exterminated by old Monkey!

TRIPITAKA:
That's a terrible thing you have done! It's true they were fearsome
robbers, but they would not have been sentenced to death even if
they had been caught and tried. If you have such vast abilities, you
should have frightened them and chased them away. Why did you
kill them all? We who have left the family should "keep ants out of
harm's way when we sweep the floor, and put shades on lamps for
love of moths"!

MONKEY:
Master, if I hadn't killed them, they would have killed you!

TRIPITAKA:

As a priest, I would rather die than practice violence. If I were killed, there would be only one of me dead, but you slaughtered six persons. How can you justify that?

MONKEY:

To tell you the truth, Master, when I was king on the Flower-Fruit Mountain five hundred years ago, I killed I don't know how many people.

TRIPITAKA:

It's precisely because you had neither scruples nor self-control that you had to undergo that ordeal of five hundred years. Now you have entered the fold of Buddhism, but if you still insist on taking life as before, you are not worthy to be a monk, nor can you go with me to the Western Heaven. You're wicked! You're wicked! You're just too wicked!

MONKEY:

If that's what you think, that I'm not worthy to be a monk, nor can I go to the Western Heaven, you needn't bother me further with these harangues! I'll leave and go back! Old Monkey's off!

[*He disappears.*]

TRIPITAKA:

That fellow! He's so unwilling to be taught. Well! Well! Well! It must be that I am destined not to have a disciple on my way after all. I might as well go on by myself.

[*He starts off.* GUANYIN *enters, disguised as a very old woman.*]

GUANYIN:

Elder, where do you come from, and why are you walking here all by yourself?

TRIPITAKA:

Your child was sent by the Great King of the land of the East to seek true scriptures from the living Buddha in the Western Heaven.

GUANYIN:

But that is one hundred and eight thousand miles away. You are all by yourself. How can you possibly think of going there?

TRIPITAKA:

Well, I did have a disciple, a rather unruly character. I scolded him a little and he disappeared to the East.

GUANYIN [*reaching into her robes*]:

I have here a gold fillet which used to belong to my son. He had been a monk for only three days when unfortunately he died. Father, since you have a disciple, let me give the fillet to you.

TRIPITAKA:

I am most grateful for your lavish gifts, but my disciple is gone.

GUANYIN:

My home is in the East; perhaps I can catch up with him on the way and persuade him to come back. But now, I have a spell which is called the True Words for Controlling the Mind, or the Tight-Fillet spell. Memorize it secretly. When your disciple comes back, give him the fillet to wear; and then if he refuses to obey you, recite the spell.

[*Music.* GUANYIN *hands* TRIPITAKA *a little scroll, then flies out of her old robes.*]

TRIPITAKA:
Lady Bodhisattva! Stay with me!

[*She is gone.* TRIPITAKA *exits.*]

TEA WITH THE DRAGON KING

[MONKEY *is having tea with the* DRAGON KING *in his lair.*]

DRAGON KING:
Yes, I'd heard that your five-hundred-year ordeal under the mountain had been completed. But if, as you say, you were assigned to follow the Tang monk to the Western Heaven, why are you heading eastward instead?

MONKEY [*laughing*]:
That Tang monk knows nothing of human nature! He'll never reach the Western Heaven. Can you imagine old Monkey walking all those years? What tedium! I just left him! Thought I'd stop off on my way home for a cup of tea.

DRAGON KING:
Thanks for coming.

[*An awkward pause.* MONKEY *notices a painting on the wall.*]

MONKEY:
What's this all about?

DRAGON KING:

It depicts the threefold presentation of shoes at Thunderclap Bridge.

MONKEY:

What's that?

DRAGON KING:

The immortal in the painting was sitting on the bridge when one of his shoes fell off into the water below. He asked a young man named Zhang Liang to fetch it, and the young man quickly did so, and even put it on the immortal's foot. But it fell off again, and then a third time. Each time Zhang Liang did not show the slightest pride or impatience but went into the cold water to fetch the shoe. For this, the immortal gave Zhang Liang a heavenly book. Zhang Liang went into the mountains, and he became enlightened.

[*Pause.*]

MONKEY:

What's your point?

DRAGON KING:

Dear Monkey, if you do not accompany the Tang monk, if you are unwilling to exercise diligence or to accept instruction, you will remain a bogus immortal after all. It is unwise to allow your pride, even if you are right, to make you lose this friend and abandon the way to the Western—

MONKEY:

Don't say one more word! I'm going!

[*He leaves the* DRAGON KING *and immediately runs into* GUANYIN.]

THE TIGHT-FILLET SPELL

GUANYIN:

You idiot addle-brained red bottom! You're supposed to be helping the Tang monk. Why aren't you with him?

MONKEY:

Relax! I just stopped in for some tea with—

GUANYIN:

I saved you from that mountain punishment, and you're not even trying to gain your merit!

MONKEY:

You call that saved? Having to walk every step of the way to the Western—

GUANYIN:

Stop talking, you harebrained ingrate! Get back!

[GUANYIN *flies away.* MONKEY *comes across* TRIPITAKA *sitting on the ground, his basket beside him. He has memorized the True Words for Controlling the Mind spell.*]

MONKEY:

Master, why aren't you on the road? What are you doing?

TRIPITAKA:

Your absence has forced me to sit here, not daring to move. And with your abilities, you can go anywhere to get some food, but I have to sit here and endure hunger. Are you comfortable with that?

MONKEY:

Master, if you're hungry, I'll go get you food.

TRIPITAKA:

Don't bother. On second thought, you could fetch me some water. There's a bowl in my bag.

[MONKEY *rummages in the basket. He holds up the golden fillet.*]

MONKEY [*excitedly*]:
What's this?

TRIPITAKA:

Hm? Oh, nothing.

MONKEY [*getting very excited*]:
Master, I am your loyal servant. If this fillet has magic powers, I ought to know.

TRIPITAKA:

Oh, all right then. Anyone who wears that fillet will be able to recite scripture without having to study at all.

MONKEY:

Can I put it on?

TRIPITAKA:

Well, it may not fit, but if it does you may wear it.

[MONKEY *puts the fillet on his head.*]

MONKEY:
It fits perfectly! Hmn. I can't get it off . . .

[TRIPITAKA *starts to chant.* MONKEY *writhes and somersaults in pain, shrieking.*]

Master! I've learned my lesson, please stop!

[TRIPITAKA *stops, and* MONKEY *draws his rod to strike him from behind, but* TRIPITAKA *starts to chant, and* MONKEY *is thrown backward in pain. Three more times* TRIPITAKA *starts and then stops his chanting suddenly, and* MONKEY *responds accordingly, hurled around whenever the chanting starts, recovering briefly when it stops. Finally he is exhausted.*]

TRIPITAKA [*rising in anger*]:
How can you be so reckless as to want to strike me?

MONKEY:
Master—!

TRIPITAKA:
Now will you listen to my instructions?

MONKEY:
Yes!

TRIPITAKA:
And never be unruly again!

MONKEY:
Never!

[MONKEY *picks up the basket, and the pilgrims resume their travel.* JADE EMPEROR *enters. Music.*]

THE COMING OF BAJIE

[*During the following,* TRIPITAKA *and* MONKEY *travel along. At one point,* MONKEY *scouts ahead and then returns.*]

JADE EMPEROR:
Traveling by day, and sleeping by night,
Clothed by the moon and drinking the wind,
Our two pilgrims made tracks in the grassy turf.
The summer fades and the light is waning;
Autumn has come again, and still they are on their way.

[JADE EMPEROR *exits. Music ends.*]

MONKEY:
Master, you may proceed. The village up ahead appears to be one of good families where we can seek shelter.

TRIPITAKA:
Very well, then . . .

[*A villager,* MR. GAO, *passes by.* MONKEY *grabs hold of him and won't let go.*]

MONKEY:
Hey, I have a question for you! What village is this?

MR. GAO:

Isn't there anyone else in the village? Why must you pick on me with your question?

MONKEY:

Patron, don't get upset: "Helping others is helping yourself."

MR. GAO:

The grievances I have suffered are not at an end, and now I have to run into this bald-headed fellow and suffer indignities from him!

TRIPITAKA [*embarrassed*]:

Pilgrim Sun, isn't someone coming over there? You can ask someone else. Let the man go.

MONKEY [*as* MR. GAO *struggles*]:

But, Master, if I let him go, I'll never know his grievances. This might be a chance for us to earn merit. Now, patron, tell me who you are and all your troubles.

MR. GAO:

All right then!

[MONKEY *lets go.*]

My name is Mr. Gao. I have a daughter who is not yet betrothed. Three years ago a monster seized her and kept her as his wife.

TRIPITAKA [*terrified*]:

A monster! Where?

MR. GAO:

Having a monster as a son-in-law is terrible! First, it has ruined the family reputation, and second, there aren't even any in-laws with whom we can be friends. I tried to have the marriage annulled, but the monster absolutely refused. I've tried to find someone to exorcise the monster, and I've turned up three or four persons—all worthless monks and impotent Daoists.

MONKEY:

Your search is at an end!

TRIPITAKA:

Pilgrim, what are you saying? Isn't it better that we just go on with our journey?

MONKEY:

Master, this is our journey! Now take us—

MR. GAO:

Don't mislead me! I've had it up to here! I already have one ugly monster in the house, I don't need another!

TRIPITAKA:

Just so, Mr. Gao; if you'll forgive us, we'll be on our way.

MONKEY:

What's all this muttering about appearances? I, old Monkey, may be ugly, but I can catch that monster for you! We're high monks on our way to the Western Heaven!

MR. GAO:
Well—

MONKEY:

Now, sit down and tell me everything about that monster: how he came to the place, what power he has, and so forth.

[*They all sit.*]

MR. GAO:

Well, when he first turned up, he said he was from Fuling Mountain and that his surname was Zhu.

TRIPITAKA:

Hog?

MR. GAO:

That's right. But he was a fairly decent looking fellow and I took him in. At first he was industrious and well behaved. He could plow the fields without even using a buffalo. The only trouble was his appearance began to change.

TRIPITAKA:

In what way?

MR. GAO:

Well, when he first came, he was a stout, swarthy fellow, but soon he began to grow huge ears and a long snout. His body became coarse and hulking. In short, he turned into a pig. And what an appetite! A meal means five bushels of rice, and a snack in the morning is over one hundred biscuits! It's a good thing he's a vegetarian or my estate would be destroyed in half a year!

TRIPITAKA:

Perhaps it's because he's a good worker that he has such an appetite.

MR. GAO:

Oh, the appetite is a small problem. What is most disturbing is that he likes to ride on the wind and disappear on the fog. He kicks up stones and dirt so much we never have a moment's peace. Then he locked up my little girl, Green Orchid, in the back building, and we haven't seen her for half a year. We don't know if she's alive or dead!

MONKEY:

Relax, we'll take care of him.

MR. GAO:

What sort of weapon do you need?

MONKEY:

None, I have one.

MR. GAO:

And followers? Do you need followers?

MONKEY:

Not at all. Now take me to this back building. Master, you stay where it's safe.

TRIPITAKA:

You're sure you don't need my help?

[He runs off. MONKEY and MR. GAO approach the door of the back building.]

MONKEY:

Now, you say there is a lock on this door?

MR. GAO:
Yes. My son-in-law must have put a spell on it. It is unbreakable.

MONKEY:
We'll see about that.

[*He blows on the lock. The door swings open.*]

Call your daughter.

MR. GAO:
Green Orchid? Are you in there?

[GREEN ORCHID *runs out and jumps into her father's arms. She has a green ornament in her hair.*]

GREEN ORCHID:
Papa!

MONKEY:
Stop all that crying! Let me ask you—where's the monster?

GREEN ORCHID:
I don't know! He leaves in the morning and only comes home late at night. He demands his five buckets of rice, and then he goes to sleep.

MONKEY:
Hm. Green Orchid, we need to switch bodies—how about it?

GREEN ORCHID:
I'll try anything if it will get rid of my big hog husband!

MONKEY:
All right then. Let's go.

[*They shake hands, vibrate, and now* MONKEY *is* GREEN ORCHID *and vice versa.* GREEN ORCHID *walks bowlegged like* MONKEY *and is full of confidence;* MONKEY *is upright but moves like a cowering little girl and speaks with a high, squeaky voice.*]

GREEN ORCHID [*inhabited by* MONKEY]:
Take her away, Mr. Gao, spend all the time you want with her.

MONKEY [*inhabited by* GREEN ORCHID]:
Papa!

[MONKEY *jumps into* MR. GAO's *arms. The wind comes up.*]

GREEN ORCHID [*inhabited by* MONKEY]:
What's this?

MONKEY [*inhabited by* GREEN ORCHID]:
He's coming, quick lock yourself in!

[MONKEY, *inhabited by* GREEN ORCHID, *is carried off by* MR. GAO. GREEN ORCHID, *inhabited by* MONKEY, *goes inside.* PIG *enters.*]

PIG:
Green Orchid! I'm home!

[*He unlocks his door and sits down outside.*]

Is my dinner ready?

[GREEN ORCHID, *inhabited by* MONKEY, *comes out with an overflowing bucket of rice, sets it down, and goes back inside.* PIG *devours the rice.*]

You seem a little annoyed with me this evening. Is it because I am late?

[GREEN ORCHID, *inhabited by* MONKEY, *comes out with another full bucket and sets it down.* PIG *starts in on it.*]

GREEN ORCHID [*inhabited by* MONKEY]:
Oh, I am so unlucky!

[*She departs with the empty bucket. Throughout the following,* GREEN ORCHID, *inhabited by* MONKEY, *continues to bring in full buckets and take out the empty ones.* PIG *keeps eating as he talks.*]

PIG:
Unlucky? It's true that I have consumed quite a bit of food and drink since I entered your family, but I certainly did not take them as free meals. Look at the things I did for your family: sweeping the grounds and draining the ditches, hauling bricks and carrying tiles, plowing the fields and raking the earth. You enjoy the flowers and fruits of four seasons, and you have fresh vegetables for the table in all eight periods. Whatever makes you so dissatisfied that you have to sigh and lament that you are unlucky?

[GREEN ORCHID, *inhabited by* MONKEY, *enters to exchange the buckets.*]

GREEN ORCHID [*inhabited by* MONKEY]:
Today my parents came and scolded me through the door, saying that a person as ugly as you is unpresentable. You've utterly ruined our family's reputation. That's why I'm upset.

[*She departs.*]

PIG:
They shouldn't judge by appearances.

GREEN ORCHID [*inhabited by* MONKEY, *calling from inside*]:
They're trying to find an exorcist to get rid of you.

PIG:
Ha! Some old Daoist I suppose.

GREEN ORCHID [*inhabited by* MONKEY, *still inside*]:
They say they've found someone really special.

PIG [*scoffing, unimpressed*]:
Oh? Who could that be?

[GREEN ORCHID, *inhabited by* MONKEY, *enters to make the last exchange of a full bucket for an empty one.*]

GREEN ORCHID [*inhabited by* MONKEY]:
The Great Sage Equal to Heaven, the Monkey King. He's a handsome, fabulous warrior who has tremendous powers. Some five hundred years ago, he even caused trouble in the Celestial Palace.

[GREEN ORCHID, *inhabited by* MONKEY, *exits.*]

PIG:

"Great Sage" . . . ? Oh, I know who you mean. That little *Bimawen*!

[MONKEY *enters in his own body, but with* GREEN ORCHID's *hair ornament still on his head. He has his golden-hooped rod with him at full size.*]

MONKEY:

What did you say?

PIG:

That little stable boy—he's nothing to—

[PIG *looks up and sees* MONKEY. *He cries out. A brief flurry during which* MONKEY *pins* PIG *to the ground with his weapon.*]

MONKEY:

Where did you hear that about me?! Talk!

PIG:

Great Sage, forgive me—

MONKEY:

Who are you? How do you know about heavenly matters?

PIG:

I too lived in Heaven once! I was the Marshal of the River of Heaven and commanded all the naval forces.

MONKEY:

You expect me to believe that, you overstuffed greaseball?

PIG:

It's the truth! But one year, at the Festival of Immortal Peaches, I had too much to drink. And I . . . I behaved improperly toward Miss Chang'e.

MONKEY:

The moon's mistress?

PIG:

She became so very annoyed with me that she filed a complaint with the Jade Emperor. He sent me down here to live out another life. But somehow things got mixed up: I ended up in an erroneous womb, and I came out like this! Now you're here to make this life miserable as well!

[MONKEY *relaxes somewhat.* TRIPITAKA *enters.*]

TRIPITAKA:

What is going on here? Is this the monster?

MONKEY:

Master, meet the overweight incarnation of the Heavenly Marshal. He took a wrong path at rebirth, but I believe his spiritual nature is not extinguished.

TRIPITAKA:

Well, scare him off! Scare him off and let us resume our westward journey.

[*He turns to go.*]

PIG:

Westward journey?! Are you the scripture pilgrim sent by the Tang Emperor?

TRIPITAKA:

I am.

PIG [*bowing to the ground*]:

Master! I am a convert of the Bodhisattva Guanyin, who commanded me to keep a vegetarian diet and wait here for the scripture pilgrim. She says that if I follow you and aid you, I may atone for my sins and live once again in the Western Heaven. I have been waiting for you for years! [*To* MONKEY] If you are his disciple why didn't you say so at once instead of unleashing violence on me at my door?

MONKEY:

If you are sincere, face Heaven and swear.

PIG:

Amitabha! Namo Buddha! If I am not speaking the truth in all sincerity, let me be chopped to bits and half of me steamed for dumplings and the other half fried up with salt!

MONKEY:

Good oath. But, Master, we cannot possibly let this idiot burden us on our westward journey.

TRIPITAKA:

Nonsense, pilgrim. If this poor convert wishes to accompany us, and the bodhisattva wills it as well, we have no choice in the matter. But we must set out again tomorrow. I fear that time is passing, and we are hardly making any progress. By the way, what shall I call you?

PIG:
The bodhisattva gave me the religious name Zhu Wuneng!

TRIPITAKA:
Good, good! Our other disciple is Wukong. But since I hear you have been keeping a strict vegetarian diet, let me call you Bajie— that is, "forbidden food."

PIG:
I shall obey my master!

EIGHT HUNDRED MILE WIDE RIVER AND TRIPITAKA'S STORY

[*Music. The* JADE EMPEROR *enters.*]

JADE EMPEROR:
And so early the next morning, after Zhu Bajie had said farewell to his wife and father-in-law, he picked up his muckrake and luggage, and the three pilgrims set out once again.

MONKEY:
Hey! Why bring along that old rake? We won't be plowing any fields soon. Don't you have enough to carry?

PIG:
For your information, this rake is not a thing of this world. It was a gift from the Jade Emperor, and it is a divine weapon.

MONKEY:

How suitable! Your weapon is a muckrake! Perfect!

TRIPITAKA:

Enough of this bickering, disciples! We must be on our way!

JADE EMPEROR:

Our three pilgrims set out upon the road.
Autumn was fading like a fire at twilight,
And the sun dropped as fast as a tired child's eyes.
Mind and body must both be tamed
If you want to reach the Western Heaven.

They traveled for a month, and the weather became unseasonably cold. Snow was falling when they came across an old, abandoned temple, perched on the very brink of an enormous river. Here our pilgrims paused.

[*Music ends.* JADE EMPEROR *exits.*]

TRIPITAKA:

Disciples, look at this vast expanse of water. Why are there no boats in sight? How can we get across?

PIG:

It's very turbulent, too rough for any boat.

TRIPITAKA:

I can't see the other shore from here. Really, how wide is it?

MONKEY:

Just about eight hundred miles.

TRIPITAKA:

Eight hundred miles?

MONKEY:

For me it would be easy to somersault over, but for you, Master, it is impossibly wide.

TRIPITAKA:

Then how will I ever get across?

[*As* TRIPITAKA *frets,* PIG *takes* MONKEY *aside.*]

PIG:

Elder Brother, if it's all so easy for you, why don't you fly and carry Master on your back?

MONKEY:

Don't you know how to ride the clouds? Can't you carry him across the river?

PIG:

You know the mortal nature and worldly bones of Master are as heavy as the Tai Mountain.

MONKEY:

And if your cloud riding can't carry him, what makes you think mine can? The proverb says, "Lift the Tai Mountain, and it's light as a mustard seed, but carry a mortal and you will never leave the red dust behind." It is required of Master to go through all these strange territories and ordeals before he finds deliverance from the sea of sorrows. When that happens, he'll be lighter than air; but until then, every step is difficult. You and I are only his protective companions, we cannot save him from his trials.

PIG:
Elder Brother, I accept your explanation amiably.

TRIPITAKA [*starting to cry*]:
Whatever shall we do?

MONKEY:
Don't cry! The moment you start to cry you already feel defeated! Right now we are together and safe in this old temple. Let old Monkey worry about the rest. Listen, Master, you know the origin of both Bajie and I, but we do not know yours. Why don't you tell us? It will take your mind off current troubles.

[*They sit. It is snowing outside the temple.*]

TRIPITAKA:
To speak the truth, for many years I had no idea of where I came from or who I was. I grew up all my life in the monastery without parents or grandparents but only the monks to teach me right from wrong. One day, when I was eighteen years old, our head priest decided it was time that I should learn who I really was. He showed me an old letter written in blood.

MONKEY:
In blood?

TRIPITAKA:
Yes, my mother's blood.

[Music. As TRIPITAKA *introduces into his story the characters of his* MOTHER, FATHER, GRANDMOTHER, *the* BOATMAN, *and* GUANYIN, *they appear upstage and in a silent, simple way enact what he describes.]*

My father was a scholar who traveled to the city to take his examinations. He did so well, he was given an appointment far out in the West. He was returning home to fetch his mother to take her with him to his new appointment, when a young girl—my mother—saw him from a window,

*[*TRIPITAKA'S MOTHER *tosses a little yellow ball to* TRIPITAKA'S FATHER.*]*

and she tossed a ball to him, to say to him,

TRIPITAKA AND TRIPITAKA'S MOTHER *[together]*:
You are the one I wish to marry.

TRIPITAKA:
My grandmother was overjoyed both that her son had passed his exams and that he had brought home a wife, and the three soon set out to my father's new appointment. But my grandmother sickened along the way, and so they let her stop at an inn and said they would be back soon to fetch her.

MONKEY:
Go on, Master, why have you stopped?

TRIPITAKA:
Well, along the way, my parents came to a river. The boatman was predestined to be my father's mortal enemy. My mother was too beautiful, and he wanted her for his own. He killed my father and

dragged my mother off. She used her own blood to write that she wanted to die, and she was on the point of suicide when Guanyin stopped her and said:

GUANYIN [*to* TRIPITAKA'S MOTHER]:
You are already with child by your husband, and your son is the eleventh incarnation of Gold Cicada, a very holy being.

TRIPITAKA:
My mother endured her life until my birth. Then, fearing that the boatman would kill me, she put me in a basket of reeds, attached her note to my clothes, and set me in a rapid stream flowing to the East. I don't know how long I drifted; it was the monks who found me.

[*Pause.*]

In the last line of her letter my mother said that now she was free to die; to join my father. And she said she intended to throw herself from a cliff into the arms of death.

MONKEY:
And do you believe she did?

[TRIPITAKA'S MOTHER *falls, and the little yellow ball rolls from her hand.*]

TRIPITAKA:
Yes, I believe she did.

[*Music ends.* PIG *has fallen asleep.*]

MONKEY:

Well, you and I have two things in common: neither of us has any parents, and Bodhisattva Guanyin has known us both for a very long time.

TRIPITAKA:

But why is it so cold? At home we would never feel such cold or see such snow at this time of year.

MONKEY:

Master, you have such longing for your home, and you think it is behind you in the East. But when we reach the Western Heaven, and you see the face of Buddha, you will know then that you are truly home.

TRIPITAKA:

What do you mean? This journey is so difficult, I haven't yet begun to plan for the way back east.

MONKEY:

It is growing colder, Master, and dark. Stay here and watch the snow fall until your own eyes drop. I'll go along the shore and investigate; perhaps there is some vessel for us there.

[MONKEY *departs.* TRIPITAKA *falls asleep as* JADE EMPEROR *enters.*]

JADE EMPEROR:

Our scripture pilgrim did as he was told and fell asleep, along with Bajie. But do not think they were alone. That river was deep as well as wide and contained someone who late at night crept up to the temple to have a look.

[*Through an opening in the temple wall, the enormous eye of a monster (*SHA MONK*) appears and gazes around for a moment then fixes on* TRIPITAKA.]

JADE EMPEROR [*aloud*]:
That monster saw the appetizing holy monk and had a thought.

[*The eye looks straight ahead then disappears. It is dawn. The snow has stopped;* MONKEY *enters.*]

MONKEY:
Wake up, Master. [*To* PIG] Wake up, Idiot! I have great news.

TRIPITAKA:
Did you find a boat to carry us across?

MONKEY:
No need for a boat, Master, this great cold has frozen the river solid. The people from the village are all crossing over to sell wares on the other side.

TRIPITAKA:
Am I so different from these people? My quest for scripture and yours for redemption are far more important than their worldly trade, and yet we stand here on the shore. Pilgrim Sun, let's make use of the ice as well and leave for the West at once. Let's hurry!

PIG:
Wouldn't it be better to rest here a few days, and see if the weather warms up? I'm hungry, and it's comfortable here and—

MONKEY:
If you want to go home, go home, you family-hugging devil!

PIG:

I never said I wanted to go home, only that it might be safer for Master to wait. This hurry may cause us to make mistakes!

TRIPITAKA:

It will only grow colder and colder from now on. If we wait, we could be delayed, perhaps even half a year.

[*Music. The pilgrims head out.*]

JADE EMPEROR:

Thus with impatience as wide as the river, those three gathered up the luggage and set out. They made their way slowly over miles of the devious ice.

[*Members of the company bring out a large piece of silver-colored silk and lay it on the ground.*]

There were snow piles rising up like hills
As sunlight broke up the clouds of dawn.
Pond fishes cuddled in the dense weeds;
Wild birds hugged the dead branches.
The whole river was one cold piece of jade
Without a ripple throughout the water's width:
It seemed a road on land, only bright, clean, and smooth.

[*Music ends. The pilgrims are on the ice.* TRIPITAKA *edges forward slowly, tapping the ice ahead of him with his walking stick.*]

TRIPITAKA:

Now you see, Bajie, if we had listened to you we would still be sitting in the temple instead of halfway over the river. This isn't really so difficult, once one is used to it. I think this goes to show that we should always hurry along as best we can and—

[*There is an ominous cracking sound.*]

What was that?

PIG:
This river is so solidly frozen that the ice must be scraping the riverbed.

TRIPITAKA:
Oh. As I was saying—

[*The ice cracks open, and* TRIPITAKA *is sucked down.* SHA MONK *appears from below. He wears a necklace of nine skulls.*]

SHA MONK:
Ha! Human flesh! There's nothing like it! I spied him sleeping in the temple last night, and I knew that I could get him! Now I have him beneath my river: How shall I eat him—steamed or fried?

[SHA MONK *laughs triumphantly. There is a tremendous sound of rushing water. He disappears, sucking down the silk cloth with him.* MONKEY *and* PIG *stare down into the hole.*]

JADE EMPEROR:
We do not know what has happened to Tripitaka Tang down under the ice, but if you want to find out, you must come back for the second act.

ACT II

ENTR'ACTE

[*The* JADE EMPEROR *is where we left him.* FISHERMAN ZHANG *is fishing.*]

JADE EMPEROR:
We were telling you about Tripitaka Tang, Sun Wukong, and Zhu Bajie and the troubles at Eight Hundred Mile Wide River. But before we return to them, let us acknowledge that a journey to the West is not for everyone. Meet Fisherman Zhang and Woodsman Li,

[WOODSMAN LI *enters.*]

two old friends, and listen for a moment to what they have to say.

WOODSMAN LI:
Good evening, Brother Zhang.

FISHERMAN ZHANG:
Good evening, Brother Li.

WOODSMAN LI:
You seem pensive, Brother Zhang.

FISHERMAN ZHANG:
Brother Li, in my opinion those who strive for fame lose their lives on account of fame; those who have titles sleep embracing a tiger; and those who receive official favors walk with snakes in their sleeves. Their lives cannot compete with ours, here near the fair waters and blue mountains.

WOODSMAN LI:
Brother Zhang, there's a great deal of truth in what you say. But you can't compare your fair waters to my blue mountains. Nothing can match them.

FISHERMAN ZHANG:
On the contrary, your blue mountains cannot match my fair waters, in testimony of which I offer a poem:

On ten thousand miles of misty waters in a tiny boat,
Surrounded by the sound of the mermaid-fish
I cast out my net and startle the stars upon the water;
They dance, they turn, and then reassemble.

WOODSMAN LI:
Marvelous, Brother Zhang. But listen to this:

In one pine-seeded corner of a dense forest,
I listen wordless to the oriole.

And at night, when I return to my home,
My head is crowned by wild blossoms,
Ruby and gold, tangled in my hair.

FISHERMAN ZHANG:
Very beautiful, Brother Li.

[*Music. Introduction to the song of* WOODSMAN LI *and* FISHERMAN ZHANG.]

WOODSMAN LI:
So far, the poems we have recited are occasional pieces, hardly anything unusual. Why don't we attempt a long poem in the linking-verse manner and see how our conversation fares?

FISHERMAN ZHANG:
That is a marvelous proposal, Brother Li! Please begin.

[*Music. The melody.* WOODSMAN LI *and* FISHERMAN ZHANG *sing the rest of their dialogue.*]

WOODSMAN LI:
A rustic man, feigning madness, loves the wind and moon.

FISHERMAN ZHANG:
An old fellow leaves his pride to the streams and lakes.

WOODSMAN LI:
Untouched by joy or sorrow, I befriend pines and plums.

FISHERMAN ZHANG:
I'm pleased to keep company with egrets and gulls.

WOODSMAN LI:

I've no plans for fame or fortune in my heart.

FISHERMAN ZHANG:

My ears have never heard the din of spears and drums.

WOODSMAN LI:

My living consists in two bundles of wood.

FISHERMAN ZHANG:

My trade is my pole with hooks and threads.

WOODSMAN LI:

When winter comes I sleep soundly though the sun is high.

FISHERMAN ZHANG:

Under the tall, hazy sky I feel no sultry heat.

WOODSMAN LI:

Throughout the year I freely roam the hills.

FISHERMAN ZHANG:

In the four seasons I row the lakes with ease.

WOODSMAN LI:

Radiant and fragrant are the flowers at my door.

FISHERMAN ZHANG:

Tranquil is the water at the head of my boat.

WOODSMAN LI:

How rare—

FISHERMAN ZHANG:
How rare—

WOODSMAN LI:
How rare—

FISHERMAN ZHANG:
How rare—

WOODSMAN LI:
the simple love of this sweet Earth.

[FISHERMAN ZHANG *and* WOODSMAN LI *depart.* PIG *and* MONKEY *enter. The music ends.*]

SHA MONK

JADE EMPEROR:
We now rejoin our two pilgrims, staring down at the hole in the ice through which their master has disappeared.

[JADE EMPEROR *exits.*]

PIG:
Master has changed his family name to Sink, and his given name is To-the-Bottom.

MONKEY:
You were in command of the naval forces, Idiot; go down and engage that monster. I'll go off to speak to the bodhisattva about this.

PIG:

All right, then. [*Calling into the hole*] This rake of mine is no garden tool from the shed! Prepare to have nine new gaping holes!

[*He leaps in.* MONKEY *tumbles off to the bamboo grove of* GUANYIN. MOKSA *is in attendance.*]

MONKEY:

Bodhisattva, your disciple Sun Wukong pays you sincere homage.

GUANYIN:

Wait outside.

MONKEY:

Bodhisattva, my master is facing a terrible ordeal—

GUANYIN:

Go out of the grove, Monkey, and wait until I come out. Patience, Monkey, patience!

MONKEY [*to* MOKSA]:

The bodhisattva seems to be all wrapped up today in her domestic affairs. Why is she not sitting at her lotus platform? Why is she not made up? Why does she look so gloomy, making bamboo baskets in the grove?

MOKSA:

We don't know. When she left the cave this morning, she went straight for the grove before she was even properly dressed. Then she told us to wait for you.

MONKEY:
For me?

GUANYIN [*coming out carrying a little basket*]:
Why aren't you with the Tang monk?

MONKEY:
He's with a monster under a river! We couldn't cross and then it froze and so we tried to hurry across with the tradesmen and it broke and the monster—it's why I've come, we—

GUANYIN:
Did you introduce yourself?

MONKEY:
To—what? Did I what?

GUANYIN:
Are you still feeling too smug and self-important to disclose the fact that you are serving the Tang monk on a westward journey?

MONKEY:
I'm not good at doing business underwater! I'm not good at introductions!

GUANYIN:
Come with me.

MONKEY:
I don't dare press you; let the bodhisattva dress and—

GUANYIN:
No need to dress, let's go.

[*They fly along.* PIG *emerges from the ice, exhausted, and sees them approach.*]

PIG:
What havoc has that Monkey stirred up in the south seas to bring the bodhisattva here undressed? Lady Bodhisattva, forgive us!

GUANYIN:
Get out of the way. [*Calling down the hole*] Wujing? Wujing?

[SHA MONK *appears from under the ice.*]

SHA MONK:
My Lady Bodhisattva!

[SHA MONK *sees* MONKEY.]

What are you doing with the stable boy?

[MONKEY *is flummoxed.*]

GUANYIN:
Never mind! Didn't I tell you to wait for a scripture pilgrim sent by the Tang Emperor?

SHA MONK:
Yes.

GUANYIN:

And didn't I tell you to accompany him to the West in order to gain merit and earn your redemption?

SHA MONK:

Yes.

GUANYIN:

Well, now you've got him, and you're threatening to steam or fry him? Do you want to remain a monster forever?

SHA MONK:

Forgive me, my Lady Bodhisattva. He did not identify himself!

GUANYIN:

Bring him up immediately; he is your new master.

[SHA MONK *disappears beneath the ice.*]

This poor monster was once the Curtain-Raising Captain of the heavenly court. But at the Festival of Immortal Peaches he broke a jade vase belonging to the emperor. He was sent down to Earth as a river monster. I see he is still good at breaking things up.

[TRIPITAKA *emerges, bound and with an apple in his mouth.* PIG *removes the apple and bites into it.* MONKEY *starts to untie him.*]

TRIPITAKA:

Lady Bodhisattva!

GUANYIN:

Tripitaka Tang, how could you confuse yourself with those who hurry over the ice for the sake of worldly trade and fortune? Rushing about is not the way to the Western Heaven. If you hurry, you will never arrive. And all of you—Sun Wukong, Bajie, and Wujing—shame on you! When will you see you must work as one to reach the Western Heaven and be redeemed?

[*The pilgrims all bow to* GUANYIN. *She addresses* SHA MONK.]

Now, take this basket I have made, surround it with those skulls of yours, and you will have a carriage to take this mortal across the ice. Monkey, I hope not to hear from you soon.

[*She flies off.*]

SHA MONK:

Master, your disciple has eyes but no pupils. I have greatly offended you, and I beg you to pardon me.

TRIPITAKA:

Are you truly willing to embrace our faith and devote yourself to the journey?

SHA MONK:

I was converted by the bodhisattva many years ago. How could I be unwilling to come with you?

TRIPITAKA:

Well then, what shall I call you?

SHA MONK:

Taking my surname from the river, the bodhisattva many years ago gave me the religious name Sha Wujing.

TRIPITAKA:

Then I shall call you Sha Monk. We must be on our way.

108,000 MILES

[*Music. The pilgrims set out. The* JADE EMPEROR *enters.*]

JADE EMPEROR:

With the basket made by Guanyin, and the nine skulls of the former monster, the pilgrims, now four in number, fashioned a dharma carriage which, pulled by Sha Monk, carried them all safely across the ice.

As they proceeded we cannot tell you in full how they rested by the waters and dined in the wind, how they were covered with frost and exposed to the dew. Master and disciples journeyed for a long time, but soon enough it was spring again.

[*Music ends.* JADE EMPEROR *exits.*]

TRIPITAKA:

Disciples, since I began this journey to the West, I have passed through many regions, all rather treacherous and difficult to traverse. None of the other places has scenery like this, which is extraordinarily beautiful. Perhaps this means we are not far from the Thunderclap Mountain of the Western Heaven, and if so, we should prepare in a dignified and solemn manner to meet the world's honored one.

MONKEY:
Oh, it is still too early, much too early!

SHA MONK:
Elder Brother, how far is it to Thunderclap Mountain?

MONKEY:
One hundred eight thousand miles, and we haven't covered a tenth the distance.

PIG:
Elder Brother, how many years do we have to travel before we get there?

MONKEY:
If we're talking about you two, this journey would take some ten days. If we're talking about me, I could make fifty round trips in a day, and there would still be sunlight. But if we're talking about Master, then don't even think about it!

TRIPITAKA:
Pilgrim, tell us when we shall reach our destination.

MONKEY:
You can walk from the time of your youth till the time you grow old and, after that, till you become youthful again; and even after going through such a cycle a thousand times, you may still find it difficult to reach the place you want to go. But when you perceive, by the resoluteness of your will, the Buddha nature in all things, and when

every one of your thoughts goes back to its very source in your memory, that will be the time you arrive at the Western Heaven.

[TRIPITAKA, *in confusion and frustration, walks ahead.*]

SHA MONK:
Pilgrim, what are you saying?

MONKEY:
I'm saying that if Master would just stand still, we'd be there.

THE WOMEN OF WESTERN LIANG

[JADE EMPEROR *enters.*]

JADE EMPEROR:
As they walked along, they came upon a small river of cool, limpid currents.

MONKEY:
There must be someone running a ferryboat in those houses.

TRIPITAKA:
It's likely, but since I haven't seen a boat I don't dare open my mouth.

PIG [*shouting at the top of his lungs*]:
Hey, ferryman! Punt your boat over here! Over here, ferryman!

[*A* FERRYWOMAN *approaches.*]

FERRYWOMAN:
If you want to cross the river, come with me.

MONKEY:
You're the one ferrying the boat?

FERRYWOMAN:
Yes.

PIG [*consternated*]:
Why is the ferryman not here? Why is the ferrywoman punting the boat?

[*The* FERRYWOMAN *smiles and shrugs.*]

TRIPITAKA:
Never mind, let's get in.

JADE EMPEROR:
The ferrywoman pushed off from the shore, and the pilgrims traveled peacefully enough across the river. On the other bank they could see a small, orderly city, with flowers in every window. They disembarked and made their way.

TRIPITAKA:
Bajie, I am thirsty. Get the alms bowl and fetch me some water from the river.

PIG [*getting the bowl from the basket*]:
I was just about to drink some myself.

JADE EMPEROR:

The master drank less than half the water, and when Idiot took the bowl back, he drank the rest in one gulp. They found their way to the West, but they had hardly gone half an hour when the scripture pilgrim began to groan.

[JADE EMPEROR *exits.*]

TRIPITAKA:

Stomachache!

PIG:

I have a stomachache too!

SHA MONK:

It must be the cold water you drank.

TRIPITAKA:

The pain is awful.

PIG:

It's awful!

MONKEY:

Master, look up ahead. That looks to be an inn in the village.

SHA MONK:

We can get some hot liquid for you there and see whether there is an apothecary around.

[*They approach the inn. Several* WOMEN *are around, staring at them in wonder, shyly.*]

WOMEN [*variously, delighted*]:
Look, it's the human seed! The human seed!

[*A lady* INNKEEPER *comes out.*]

INNKEEPER:
Human seed is here!

MONKEY:
Dear lady! This poor monk has come from the land of the East.
Because he drank some water from the river back there, he is having
a stomachache.

INNKEEPER:
You drank from the river?

TRIPITAKA [*groaning*]:
Yes.

INNKEEPER:
East of here?

TRIPITAKA:
Yes!

INNKEEPER [*to all the pilgrims*]:
Come here, all of you. I'll tell you something.

MONKEY:
Dear lady, please make some hot liquid for my master—

INNKEEPER [*to the* WOMEN]:
Come on over, everyone, and look!

MONKEY:
Enough of this! Boil some water quickly!

INNKEEPER:
O Father! Boiling water is useless. Listen, this is the nation of Western Liang. There are only women in our country; until now not a single man has ever been seen here. That water your master drank is not the best, for the river is called Child-and-Mother River. Only after reaching her twentieth year would one of us go and taste that river's water, for soon after she took a drink she would feel the pain of conception. Your master has become pregnant and will give birth to a child. How could hot water cure him?

TRIPITAKA:
O disciple, what shall we do?

PIG [*frantic*]:
We are men, and we have to give birth to babies? Where can we find a birth canal? How can it come out?

MONKEY [*very amused*]:
According to the ancients, "A ripe melon will fall by itself." When the time comes, you may have a gaping hole at your armpit, and the baby will crawl out.

PIG:
Finished! Finished! I'm dead! I'm dead!

SHA MONK:

Second Elder Brother, stop writhing! You'll hurt the baby.

TRIPITAKA:

Elder Brother, please find us a midwife who is not too heavy-handed.
The movement is becoming more frequent!

SHA MONK:

Be still! You'll break your water!

MONKEY:

Dear lady, do you have a physician here? I'll ask for a prescription.

INNKEEPER:

Even drugs are useless. There is only one remedy: Due south of here
is the Male-Undoing Mountain. In it there is a cave, and inside the
cave there is a conception-free well. A little water from that well will
dissolve your problem straightaway.

MONKEY:

Excellent! Excellent! Let's go.

INNKEEPER:

But I must warn you that the guardian of that stream is an old Daoist who can be difficult.

TRIPITAKA:

What are we going to do?

MONKEY:

Relax, Master. Sha Monk and I can handle any old Daoist. Come on,
Brother, let's mount the clouds.

TRIPITAKA:
Hurry!

PIG:
Hurry!

[PIG *and* TRIPITAKA *stumble off.* MONKEY *and* SHA MONK *take off flying.*]

SHA MONK:
What do you suppose that lady could have meant by "difficult"?

MONKEY:
I don't know, but whatever it is, old Monkey can handle it. There it is: the Male-Undoing Mountain.

[*They land.*]

Perhaps it would be better if you wait and listen outside the cave, Brother, and let old Monkey determine what kind of person this guardian is.

[SHA MONK *hangs back, listening and keeping an eye on things, as* MONKEY *enters the cave. There is a creepy old* DAOIST GUARDIAN *and a bucket sitting next to the well.*]

DAOIST GUARDIAN:
Where did you come from? For what purpose have you come to this holy shrine?

MONKEY:
This poor monk is a scripture pilgrim accompanying the Tang monk from the land of the East. My master mistakenly drank from the

Child-and-Mother River, and now he is suffering from a swollen belly and unbearable pain.

DAOIST GUARDIAN:
You are accompanying the Tang monk?

MONKEY:
Yes.

DAOIST GUARDIAN:
And you say you are a Buddhist monk yourself?

MONKEY:
Yes, I was converted by the Bodhisattva Guanyin and the Buddha himself.

DAOIST GUARDIAN:
You feel you are accomplished in all the magic arts?

MONKEY:
I have extensive Daoist training.

DAOIST GUARDIAN:
Then let me challenge you to a contest. If you win, you may take all the water you want; if I win, I will return with you to your monk and devour him. For I hear that he is a reincarnation of Gold Cicada, and one bite of his holy flesh gives a thousand years of longevity.

MONKEY:
Agreed. In what realm of training do you wish to challenge me?

DAOIST GUARDIAN:
The art of sitting still.

MONKEY:
Sitting still?

DAOIST GUARDIAN:
What's the matter, Monkey, can't you do it?

MONKEY:
Of course I can! Of course! But whoever moves first—for any reason—he is the loser, agreed?

DAOIST GUARDIAN:
Agreed.

MONKEY:
Let's go.

[*They sit. Time passes. For* MONKEY, *it is excruciating. Then* SHA MONK *appears, strolls up to the well, and, as the* DAOIST GUARDIAN *looks on helplessly, enraged but unable to make a move to prevent him, he lowers the bucket into the well and pulls up some water. As* SHA MONK *signals to* MONKEY, *the* DAOIST GUARDIAN *lunges for him, and* MONKEY *and* SHA MONK *make their escape with the water.* GUANYIN *enters.*]

GUANYIN:
That old Daoist was so disgusted with himself for being tricked that he threw himself into the well and dissolved.

[*The* DAOIST GUARDIAN *tosses himself into the well.* PIG *and* TRIPI-TAKA *enter. Both are heavy with child.*]

PIG:
What do you want, a boy or a girl?

TRIPITAKA:
Stop this joking!

PIG:
I'm not joking!

[SHA MONK *and* MONKEY *fly in.*]

TRIPITAKA:
Oh, they're back! They're back! Do you have the water?

MONKEY:
Sha has it. Go on, and drink it quick!

GUANYIN:
Remember that we are born with no ideas and that everything from that moment on is just false conception. The pilgrims drank that pure well water. Worldly conception was dissolved, and their stomachs flattened out.

THE BRAMBLES OF PHILOSOPHY

[*Music. Several* WOMEN *of Western Liang appear briefly during the following and bid the pilgrims farewell.*]

GUANYIN [*continuing*]:

The pilgrims had their travel rescript certified by the women of the Liang Territory, who were very sorry to see them go. But leaving those women behind, we tell you instead about the master and his three disciples who headed toward the West. The seasons were quick to change. It was neither too hot nor too cold; it was a pleasant time to travel.

[GUANYIN *exits. The pilgrims travel until they come across an enormous pile of brambles. Music ends.*]

TRIPITAKA:

Disciples, how can we continue on this road?

MONKEY:

Why shouldn't we?

TRIPITAKA:

Don't you see it's all overgrown with brambles and clogged with prickly vines? Only insects creeping on the ground could get through.

PIG:

Don't worry, Master. Stand aside and let me show you what I can do with my rake! Don't speak of crawling on the ground; you could ride through in a carriage when I'm done.

[MONKEY *jumps on* SHA MONK's *shoulders to get a distant view.*]

TRIPITAKA:

I wonder how long this ridge is.

MONKEY:

Master, it's enormous! It must be a thousand miles long! I can't see the end of it.

SHA MONK:

Don't worry, Master. Let's follow the example of those who burn off the land and set fire to the brambles.

PIG:

Stop babbling! Now is not the season to burn the land! It's growing luxuriantly.

MONKEY [*jumping down*]:
Even if we could, the flame would burn up Master.

TRIPITAKA [*near tears*]:
How are we to get across them?

PIG:
You'll have to follow me.

[PIG *begins to hack away at the brambles.* SHA MONK *and* MONKEY *join in a bit, all to little avail.* JADE EMPEROR *enters.*]

JADE EMPEROR:

That whole day they did not rest, but raked their way as best they could. Well, what man has not met some brambles during his life?

[PIG's *clearing frenzy is diminishing.*]

TRIPITAKA:

Oh, disciple! We've tired you out! Let's spend the night here, and we'll journey again when it's light tomorrow.

PIG [*still hacking away, exhausted*]:

Don't stop now! While the sky is still fair and we're inspired, we should clear the path through the night and get on with it.

TRIPITAKA:

No, I think we have to rest now. Oh, disciples, I have such a pain in my head!

MONKEY:

Master, this place portends more evil than good. We shouldn't stay here long.

SHA MONK:

Elder Brother, aren't you overly suspicious? There's no one dangerous here, let alone a weird beast or fiendish bird. What's there to be afraid of?

[*An enormous wind. The disciples and* TRIPITAKA *cry out after one another, but the three disciples are blown away, leaving* TRIPITAKA *alone. Four extremely* AGED IMMORTALS, *named* EIGHT-AND-TEN, LONESOME RECTITUDE, CLOUD-BRUSHING DEAN, *and* MASTER VOID-SURMOUNTING, *come tottering in, leaning on knotty canes. Aged, decrepit* ATTENDANTS *bear trays of teacups and scrolls of poetry. It takes everyone a long time to arrive and settle down. They speak in their creaking voices as they approach.*]

EIGHT-AND-TEN:

Sage Monk, please don't be afraid. We are not bad people. I have brought you here on a gale of wind to meet a few friends and talk about poetry.

CLOUD-BRUSHING DEAN:

Squire Eight-and-Ten has succeeded in inviting the Sage Monk here!

TRIPITAKA:

What merit or virtue does this disciple possess that he should win such kind attention from these aged immortals?

EIGHT-AND-TEN:

We have always heard that the Sage Monk is possessed of the Way. We have waited for you for a long time. We beg you to sit and chat with us, as we long to know the true teachings.

TRIPITAKA:

May I know the names of the honorable immortals?

EIGHT-AND-TEN:

This is Squire Lonesome Rectitude, this is Master Void-Surmounting, and this is Cloud-Brushing Dean. This old moron bears the name Eight-and-Ten.

TRIPITAKA:

What age have you attained?

LONESOME RECTITUDE:

A thousand.

MASTER VOID-SURMOUNTING:
A thousand.

CLOUD-BRUSHING DEAN:
A thousand.

EIGHT-AND-TEN:
We beg you to give us your thoughts on the rudiments of the law of Zen. It would gratify our lifelong desire.

TRIPITAKA:
Zen is quiescence, and the law is salvation. But the salvation of quiescence will not be accomplished without enlightenment. The cleansing of the body and the mind and the purgation of desires, the abandonment of the worldly and departure from the dust—that is enlightenment.

LONESOME RECTITUDE:
Wonderful.

MASTER VOID-SURMOUNTING:
Marvelous.

CLOUD-BRUSHING DEAN:
Fascinating.

EIGHT-AND-TEN:
More thought, more thought!

ALL [*variously*]:
Yes, more thought, more thought!

TRIPITAKA:

Well . . .

JADE EMPEROR:

And so it went on, hour after hour, the master expounding on the law and the Little Vehicle, and those aged immortals hanging on every word. Late into the night, they were joined by a beautiful immortal girl.

EIGHT-AND-TEN:

To what do we owe this visit, Apricot Immortal?

APRICOT:

I learned that a charming guest is being entertained here. May I meet him?

EIGHT-AND-TEN:

Please take a seat.

APRICOT:

You are reveling in great pleasures this evening. May I be instructed a little by your excellent thoughts and verses?

TRIPITAKA:

Why certainly.

JADE EMPEROR:

And with that, the lively discourse began anew. They talked on into the night; first Tripitaka would offer a poem, and then the Apricot Immortal would offer her composition in reply. When they grew weary, the attendants refreshed them. They talked so long, in fact,

[GUANYIN *enters.*]

that only the sound of a rooster

[GUANYIN *crows like a rooster.*]

sent by the Bodhisattva Guanyin, brought the scripture pilgrim to his senses.

[GUANYIN *exits.*]

TRIPITAKA:
Good heavens. My friends, it is morning already. I have three loyal disciples who must be quite worried. If I may beg my leave of you, honored friends, I will be on my way.

APRICOT:
Sage Monk, your compositions come from a mind of silk and a mouth of brocade. Please grant me another.

TRIPITAKA:
Dear mistress and aged sirs, your humble monk has an appointment in the West, and he cannot linger even a single day, although here the hours seem to pass like seconds.

APRICOT [*coquettishly*]:
Why run off, charming guest? Is there something else we might offer you?

TRIPITAKA:
Perhaps I am a bit confused . . .

EIGHT-AND-TEN:
If the Apricot Immortal has such genial feelings, how could the Sage Monk not give his consent? He doesn't know how lucky he is.

[*The* AGED IMMORTALS *all chuckle.*]

TRIPITAKA [*very embarrassed*]:
My friends, if I did not know better I would almost think that this distinguished group of elders was using this young coquette to seduce me—

AGED IMMORTALS [*variously, gasping*]:
No! Oh, heavens no!

EIGHT-AND-TEN:
Oh, well, now you've made her cry . . .

TRIPITAKA:
Forgive me, gentle mistress. Forgive my impolite outburst—

APRICOT:
Clearly the holy monk does not consider me worthy of even a poem!

TRIPITAKA:
Please don't be so upset. Listen, listen:

A young face, kingfisher adorned
And colors better than—

[*A tremendous noise of wind and shouting.* MONKEY, SHA MONK, *and* PIG *burst in, brandishing their weapons. The* AGED IMMORTALS *cower in terror.*]

MONKEY:
Master, at last!

PIG:
Stand back, Master, I'll smash these toothless geezers into match-sticks!

SHA MONK:
We'll save you, Master!

TRIPITAKA:
Disciples, stop! Put down your weapons! These are not monsters or villains. They are dear and honored friends. I have spent a most blessed evening in their company.

MONKEY:
An evening?

TRIPITAKA:
Yes, we discussed the Dao and composed verses until the sun came up.

MONKEY:
Master, you have been gone an entire year!

[*Pause.*]

TRIPITAKA:
That's impossible.

[*The* AGED IMMORTALS *hang their heads.*]

PIG:
It's true, Master.

SHA MONK:
Summer came, and fall and winter and finally spring again. We searched the forests and the hills night and day, but still we couldn't find you.

TRIPITAKA:
Impossible . . .

MONKEY:
These friends of yours, Master, may look like reverend elders to you. But as one who has studied the magic arts of transformation, I would know five demon tree spirits anywhere.

TRIPITAKA [to the AGED IMMORTALS]:
Is it true?

EIGHT-AND-TEN:
Dear Monk. Please don't think badly of us. The Great Sage is right. We are the Sylvan Immortals of Bramble Ridge. I am the pine tree spirit.

LONESOME RECTITUDE:
I am the cypress.

MASTER VOID-SURMOUNTING:
I am the juniper.

CLOUD-BRUSHING DEAN:
I am the bamboo.

EIGHT-AND-TEN:
For a thousand years we have stood together on a nearby cliff, waiting for an interesting visitor to come along so we could talk philosophy.

TRIPITAKA:
But you tricked me—

LONESOME RECTITUDE:
Didn't you enjoy yourself?

CLOUD-BRUSHING DEAN:
Such delightful conversation . . .

MASTER VOID-SURMOUNTING:
Such pleasant verses and thoughts . . .

MONKEY:
Master, you have been caught in the brambles of too much thinking and the tangled vines of talking; you will never reach the Western Heaven that way.

TRIPITAKA:
But I was thinking and talking about the law of Buddha—

MONKEY:
Too much thinking! Too much thinking!

PIG [*to the* AGED IMMORTALS]:
Now get out of here! Go on back to your cliff before I chop you into kindling to cook my evening meal!

EIGHT-AND-TEN:
We're going, we're going. Forgive us, Holy Sage.

[*They teeter off.*]

JADE EMPEROR:
And with that, the path to the West was clear and untangled again. Those old trees crept back into the forest, where they may stand forever discoursing with the empty wind.

HEARTS OF DESIRE

[*Music. The pilgrims travel.*]

JADE EMPEROR:
The purpose of this next scene is to demonstrate that although the monsters we meet on the journey to the West are nothing more than the obstacles of our own personality, still they may be more fierce and vicious than the wildest wild creatures you would ever care to meet.

[JADE EMPEROR *exits. The pilgrims are entering a new city. Music ends. An* OFFICER *approaches.*]

OFFICER:
Holy Monk!

MONKEY:
What is the name of this region?

OFFICER:

Elder, pardon me! This place used to be called Bhiksu Kingdom, but it has been changed now to Young Masters' City.

TRIPITAKA:

Why should they change the name?

PIG:

They must call it Young Masters' City because "Bhiksu" is too hard to pronounce.

TRIPITAKA:

Thank you, Bajie. We can make further inquiries inside the city. Officer, where is the monastery?

OFFICER:

Just up ahead. But, Holy Monks, follow my advice and don't make any inquiries.

[OFFICER *exits.*]

TRIPITAKA:

What a peculiar fellow!

PIG:

Master, look. This must be an auspicious day for marriages. Almost every house has put a geese coop outside its front door.

MONKEY:

What an idiot! How could every household be having a wedding?

PIG:
I don't know.

MONKEY:
Master, there's the monastery up ahead. Younger brothers, accompany the Tang monk there while old Monkey investigates.

TRIPITAKA:
Very well then.

[MONKEY *scampers off. The remaining pilgrims are greeted by a* MONK *at the door of the monastery.*]

MONK:
Holy Brother, you are welcome. Please sit, and we'll prepare a vegetarian meal for you.

PIG:
I can't wait. Which way is the kitchen?

MONK:
It's—

PIG [*shoving past the* MONK]:
Never mind, I can find it.

TRIPITAKA:
Do you think it is possible for me to enter court this evening? I must have my travel rescript certified.

MONK:
You can't do it tonight. You'd better wait until early court tomorrow.

[*The* MONK *exits as* MONKEY *returns.*]

MONKEY:
Master, you may not believe your disciple, but inside every one of those geese coops there is a child. Some are playing in the coop, others merely sit and cry, and some are eating fruit or sleeping. There are hundreds of them.

[*The* MONK *returns with two bowls of rice and hands them to* TRIPITAKA *and* SHA MONK.]

MONK:
Your other disciple has a . . . healthy appetite.

TRIPITAKA:
Yes, he does. Thank you, sir. There is something this humble cleric must ask you to explain. We have seen that there is a geese coop in front of every dwelling of the city, and that each one contains a little child. May I ask, why is that?

MONK:
Elder, don't mind that! Don't ask about that! Please eat and then rest, and you can be on your way tomorrow.

TRIPITAKA:
No, I insist that you tell me.

MONK:
Elder, be careful what you say!

MONKEY [threatening]:
Old Monk, if you value your life, tell the master what he wants to know!

[TRIPITAKA begins the True Words for Controlling the Mind spell, and MONKEY begins to shriek and grasp his head. The old MONK is astonished.]

MONK:
All right, then! All right! The matter of the geese coops is caused by the befuddlement of our king.

TRIPITAKA:
Befuddlement?

[As the MONK begins his tale, the KING, the DAOIST FATHER-IN-LAW, and a GIRL enter. The two scenes share the stage.]

MONK:
Three years ago, an old man calling himself a Daoist arrived at our city with a young girl, barely sixteen, with a face as beautiful as Guanyin's. He presented her as a tribute to His Majesty. The instant our king saw her, his heart began to clamor like a hundred buckets in a single well; he lost his senses, and the whole world fell away.

[Music, a strange, sensual, and melancholy tune. The KING falls immediately under the spell of the GIRL. He embraces her, lies on the floor with her. Throughout the following scene, he does not leave the stage. Every time he seems to come to his senses and seems about to leave the GIRL, he looks at her and rejoins her. The GIRL is perpetually lounging there. The DAOIST FATHER-IN-LAW whispers in his ear.]

DAOIST FATHER-IN-LAW:
There is nothing else but her.

MONK:
They say he can't remember who he is.

DAOIST FATHER-IN-LAW:
Look to her; the answer is in her.

MONK:
The old Daoist has been appointed royal father-in-law. He sits by the king's shoulder every day.

KING [*stirring*]:
I need to go outside.

DAOIST FATHER-IN-LAW:
There's nothing there.

MONK:
And every day he whispers to the king,

DAOIST FATHER-IN-LAW:
There's nothing there.

KING:
I need to address the people.

DAOIST FATHER-IN-LAW:
They don't care what you say.

KING:
I want to see the sun.

DAOIST FATHER-IN-LAW:
Look into her eyes.

MONK:
He has come to believe there is no other happiness

DAOIST FATHER-IN-LAW:
There is no other happiness.

MONK:
than in that darkened room with her.

KING:
I want to go—

DAOIST FATHER-IN-LAW:
What?

KING [*with increasing weakness*]:
I want to—

DAOIST FATHER-IN-LAW:
Yes?

KING:
I want—

[*He falls back into the arms of the* GIRL.]

MONK:

Constantly fatigued, unable to eat or drink, our king does not have long to live. The royal father-in-law, who is, in truth, the cause of this disease, claims to know a cure.

TRIPITAKA:

Oh, no.

DAOIST FATHER-IN-LAW:

Beloved son-in-law, there is a simple cure for what ails you. You only need the hearts of one thousand one hundred and eleven boys. With the soup I'll make from those, you will live a thousand years; and every day and night may be spent here with my daughter.

[*Music ends.*]

TRIPITAKA:

How horrible!

MONK:

Those tender hearts are to be the medicine. The people are forbidden even to weep for their children, but in their sorrow they renamed our city the Young Masters' City.

TRIPITAKA:

So this poor king is ill with desire. Even so, how can he think of taking the lives of so many innocents?

MONK:

Elder, there is nothing to be done. When you go to court tomorrow, confine your business to certifying your travel rescript. Don't mention this matter at all. Now good night.

[*The* MONK *exits.*]

TRIPITAKA:
Good night. My disciples, I have such a pain here in my heart.

MONKEY:
Master, what's the matter with you? You're always picking up someone else's coffin and crying over it in your own house!

TRIPITAKA:
How can you be so hard-hearted? I've never heard of such nonsense that eating people's hearts can lengthen one's life! How could I not grieve?

SHA MONK:
Do not grieve just yet, Master. The children are still alive.

TRIPITAKA:
I am going to attend early court tomorrow.

MONKEY:
Master, let old Monkey go with you.

TRIPITAKA:
But Pilgrim Sun, you always refuse to perform the proper ceremony—you won't bow to anyone. The king may be offended and refuse to sign our rescript.

MONKEY:
Then I will go with you in some hidden way.

TRIPITAKA:
So be it.

[*The pilgrims exit. Music begins.*]

KING:
Where is she?

[*He has the* GIRL *in his arms.*]

DAOIST FATHER-IN-LAW:
She's right here.

KING:
I need to prepare for early court.

DAOIST FATHER-IN-LAW:
No, you don't.

KING:
Where is she?

DAOIST FATHER-IN-LAW:
I'll leave you alone.

[DAOIST FATHER-IN-LAW *withdraws. Music ends. An* ATTENDANT *enters with* TRIPITAKA. MONKEY *is hidden in the rafters.*]

ATTENDANT:
Majesty, there is a monk here from the East. He wishes to have his travel rescript certified.

[ATTENDANT *exits.*]

KING:
Who are you?

TRIPITAKA:
My name is Tripitaka; I am on a pilgrimage to seek holy scriptures in the West.

KING:
What?

TRIPITAKA:
I wish to have my rescript certified.

KING:
Who let you in?

TRIPITAKA:
I was announced.

KING:
Oh. Where is she?

TRIPITAKA:
Please—

KING:
I'll authorize the rescript. Now leave me—

[ATTENDANT *reenters, followed by the* DAOIST FATHER-IN-LAW.]

ATTENDANT:
The royal father-in-law has entered the court.

[*The* KING *bows down, subservient.*]

KING:
We are delighted that the royal father-in-law has honored us with his divine presence.

DAOIST FATHER-IN-LAW:
Where'd this monk come from?

KING:
He's from the land of the East; he's on a journey to the West.

TRIPITAKA:
To the Western Heaven.

DAOIST FATHER-IN-LAW:
The Western Heaven? That's a colossal waste of time. What's so good about a journey to the Western Heaven?

TRIPITAKA:
Since ancient times, the West has been the noble region of ultimate bliss.

DAOIST FATHER-IN-LAW:
Tell me, I heard once that monks are the disciples of Buddha and that they can transcend even death.

TRIPITAKA:
First, they must transcend desire.

KING:
How do they do that?

DAOIST FATHER-IN-LAW:
Your mouth, Monk, is full of garbage. Those within your fold all talk about the knowledge of reality, but you don't know the first thing about reality, with your eyes closed and your hands folded day in and day out. As the proverb says, "Sit, sit, sit! Your ass will split!" Don't listen to him, beloved son-in-law, you'll have your longevity soon enough.

KING:
Thank you, Noble Father-in-Law.

TRIPITAKA:
Farewell.

[TRIPITAKA *exits.* MONKEY *remains, hidden.*]

DAOIST FATHER-IN-LAW:
Son-in-law, Heaven has sent you a gift.

KING:
Have the hearts been collected?

DAOIST FATHER-IN-LAW:
That monk is worth ten times ten thousand hearts. I saw straight-away he is a true body, one that has practiced religion for at least ten incarnations, and that he has been a monk since childhood. One bite of his flesh, and you will live ten thousand years.

KING:

Why didn't you tell us sooner? I would have detained him.

DAOIST FATHER-IN-LAW:

But that's not difficult. Have that monk arrested and ask for his heart politely. Promise him an imperial shrine and perpetual sacrifice. If he agrees, cut him up and take it out at once.

[MONKEY *has heard enough. He sneaks out.*]

If he doesn't comply, we'll cut him up just the same. Isn't that easy?

KING:

Where is she?

DAOIST FATHER-IN-LAW:

She's right here.

[MONKEY *meets* TRIPITAKA *at the monastery.*]

MONKEY:

Master, that so-called royal father-in-law is a monster spirit. He wants those hearts collected for himself and for that girl, and the king is just the way to do it. Now he wants yours as well.

TRIPITAKA:

My heart? O worthy disciple, how will we face this?

MONKEY:

No time for talk. The old must become the young.

TRIPITAKA:
Whatever do you mean?

MONKEY:
If you want to preserve your life, the master will have to become the disciple, and the disciple the master.

TRIPITAKA:
All right then.

[TRIPITAKA *and* MONKEY *grasp hands and vibrate. Now* MONKEY *is inside the body of* TRIPITAKA, *and* TRIPITAKA *inside the body of* MONKEY. TRIPITAKA *walks a bit like a monkey, and a tail peeks out from under his robes. An* ATTENDANT *enters.*]

ATTENDANT:
Holy Monk, it is our duty to bring you to the court.

TRIPITAKA [*inhabited by* MONKEY]:
Very well then.

[MONKEY, *inhabited by* TRIPITAKA, *departs.* TRIPITAKA, *inhabited by* MONKEY, *follows the* ATTENDANT *to court. The* DAOIST FATHER-IN-LAW *and* GIRL *are there with the* KING.]

KING:
An illness has afflicted us for many days, and no cure has been found. Fortunately our royal father-in-law has bestowed on me a prescription, for which only one thing is lacking—something that you have.

TRIPITAKA [*inhabited by* MONKEY]:
I came here with no possessions at all. What sort of thing do you need from me?

KING:
We need your heart. Will you give it to us?

TRIPITAKA [*inhabited by* MONKEY]:
To tell the truth, Your Majesty, I have quite a few hearts. Which color or shape would you like?

DAOIST FATHER-IN-LAW:
Priest, we want your desiring heart.

TRIPITAKA [*inhabited by* MONKEY]:
In that case, bring me the knife quickly, so that I may cut open my chest. If I have a desiring heart, I'll be pleased to give it to you.

[*The* ATTENDANT *hands* TRIPITAKA, *inhabited by* MONKEY, *a large knife. He takes the knife, seems to cut open his own chest, and hearts begin to spill out.*]

Here they are: a red heart, a white heart, a yellow heart, an avaricious heart, a petty heart, a competitive heart, an ambitious heart, a scornful heart, a murderous heart, a vicious heart, a fearful heart, a cautious heart, a nameless, obscure heart, all kinds of wicked hearts, but I have no desiring heart.

DAOIST FATHER-IN-LAW:
What kind of magic is this?

KING:
Take them away! Take them away!

TRIPITAKA [*inhabited by* MONKEY]:
Your Majesty, you have no perception at all; the heart you need lies in the chest of that man.

DAOIST FATHER-IN-LAW:
You aren't the Tang monk! Get out of here! Get out!

[TRIPITAKA, *inhabited by* MONKEY, *takes the golden-hooped rod from behind his ear and throws it on the ground.*]

TRIPITAKA [*inhabited by* MONKEY]:
Change!

[*The rod flies up, full-size.* TRIPITAKA, *inhabited by* MONKEY, *chases the* DAOIST FATHER-IN-LAW *out of the room.*]

KING [*befuddled, lost*]:
Where is she?

[*The* DAOIST FATHER-IN-LAW *dashes back in, pursued by* MONKEY *in his own form, brandishing his weapon. The* DAOIST FATHER-IN-LAW *grabs the* GIRL *and holds her in front of himself.*]

DAOIST FATHER-IN-LAW:
It's her! She's the one! It's her fault! It's her!

MONKEY:
You're nothing but a perverse fiend and deviate!

DAOIST FATHER-IN-LAW:
How dare you come here and oppress me!

[*He runs off with the* GIRL, *pursued by* MONKEY. TRIPITAKA, *in his own form,* SHA MONK, *and* PIG *run in.*]

TRIPITAKA:
Pilgrim, what has happened?

[MONKEY *reenters, carrying two large dead rats.*]

MONKEY:
Nothing at all, Master. Old Monkey's only exterminated a couple of rats.

KING:
Where is she?

MONKEY [*tossing the rats at his feet*]:
Here's your beauty and her noble father.

KING:
Where—?

TRIPITAKA:
Your Majesty, you must open your eyes. That girl and her father were nothing but rodent spirits come to steal your life from you. They were the ones who needed those hearts, not you. But you needn't worry now. My disciple has destroyed her.

KING:
Is she hurt?

TRIPITAKA:

Your Majesty, she is dead.

KING:

What do you mean? Is she coming home soon?

MONKEY:

Master, never mind him.

TRIPITAKA:

May we release those children in the geese coops?

KING:

What children? Who cares about—? Where is she?

TRIPITAKA:

Your Majesty—

[*The befuddled* KING *wanders off.*]

MONKEY:

Master, forget him. There are some born on this Earth that were never meant to live on this Earth; they cling to shadows and stare down into holes. They think happiness resides somewhere outside themselves. They don't know what it is to be awake and look around. There's nothing you can do.

THE WORLD AS A ROOM

[*The pilgrims sit. All but* MONKEY *are weary and despondent.*]

TRIPITAKA:

O disciple, why is it so difficult to reach the Western Heaven? Since leaving the city Chang'an, spring has come and gone on this road several times, autumn has arrived, followed by winter—at least four or five times. Why haven't we reached our destination?

MONKEY:

It's too early! It's too early! We haven't even passed the door of the house yet!

PIG:

Stop lying, Elder Brother! There's no such big mansion in this world.

MONKEY:

Brother, we are just moving around in one of the halls inside.

SHA MONK:

Elder Brother, stop talking so big to scare us. Where could you find such a huge house? You wouldn't be able to find crossbeams that were long enough.

PIG:

That's right!

MONKEY:

Brothers, from the point of view of old Monkey, this blue sky is our roof, the sun and moon are our windows, the mountains are the pillars, and the hands of Buddha are the walls. The whole of Heaven and Earth is one large room.

PIG:

All right, then! Why don't you move around some more in the room, and we'll go on back home and get something to eat!

TRIPITAKA:

Disciples, this journey is a serious matter. Let's be on our way.

THE PARADE OF DEMONS

[*Music. The* JADE EMPEROR *enters. As he describes the journey, there are quick little enactments of all its parts. The entire stage is filled with the adventure:* DEMONS *come from all entrances; the pilgrims split up and reunite; the adventures overlap.*]

JADE EMPEROR:

Master and disciples traveled on through many years, and because Tripitaka Tang was so full of fear and anxiety, they continued to meet monsters on their way. They encountered the yellow robe fiend who tried to steal the holy cassock and alms bowl; they encountered the cave bear spirit and white bone demon. Monkey once tried to draw a circle around the master to keep him safe, but the master was tempted outside. He encountered beautiful girls who turned out to be nothing more than spider spirits and spent a lot of time trapped by them and other monsters. He hung in the air while everyone was looking for him, or was kept in a box below the Earth. One time the pilgrims were quarreling so strenuously that Monkey split into two monkeys, and no one could tell them apart. Once they met a ghost king who had been drowned in a well, and Monkey persuaded Pig that the corpse was really a treasure. They came to a mountain that was all on fire, but Monkey found a fan large enough to put it out. Sha Monk fought bravely; Pig ate heartily; Monkey rescued the master over and over. The years slipped by like a flowing stream, and as they did, it seemed the demons became less and less formidable. And then one night, they stopped at an inn.

THE INN

[*Music ends. The parade of demons is over. The* DEMONS *are gone, and it is evening. The moon is shining brightly.* TRIPITAKA *is alone.*]

JADE EMPEROR [*continuing*]:
In exchange for performing a few simple tasks, they were allowed to stay the night. Late in the evening, Tripitaka stepped outside to relieve himself and he saw the moon.

TRIPITAKA:
Disciples, come and look.

[SHA MONK, MONKEY, *and* PIG *come out of the inn.*]

JADE EMPEROR:
Moved by that bright pure light illuminating the great Earth, he composed a poem.

TRIPITAKA:
The bright soul above hangs like a jeweled glass,
Her radiance pervades this quiet night;
She lays her soft hand on rich and poor alike—
When will she join me to return to our home?

MONKEY:
The moon is a map; she guides us on our way.

141

SHA MONK:
The moon is the hope of redemption one day.

PIG [*with great effort*]:
The moon is the color of rice, or milk.
Round as a beautiful large white cake
I'd eat it whole in the blink of an eye
If I could just pull it down with my nine-pronged rake.

TRIPITAKA:
All right, disciples, you must be tired from all this journeying. Go on to sleep. I'm going to meditate on this roll of scripture.

[*A very old woman,* GRANDMOTHER, *comes forward from the inn. She moves awkwardly toward* TRIPITAKA.]

GRANDMOTHER:
My son?

PIG [*brandishing his rake*]:
Watch out, Master!

TRIPITAKA:
Don't strike! Pilgrims, stand back!

GRANDMOTHER:
My son? My son?

PIG:
Master, this may be some demon—

TRIPITAKA:
Stand back!

GRANDMOTHER:
My son, it is your voice . . .

[*She touches* TRIPITAKA's *face.*]

How can your face still be so smooth? It's thirty years since I fell sick and you left me at the inn. I've waited and looked for you every day; I narrowed my eyes to the horizon until I went blind, but still you never came. Where have you been, my son? I dreamed you were sleeping in a river, and your wife was flying in the air . . .

TRIPITAKA:
Grandmother?

GRANDMOTHER:
Oh. I understand. I understand. How like my son you are. But where are they—my son and his beautiful wife? You know they met when she threw a ball to him. A yellow ball . . .

[TRIPITAKA *helps her to the ground and sits.*]

TRIPITAKA:
They are safe at home.

GRANDMOTHER:
Then they have forgotten me?

TRIPITAKA:

No. No. I think a demon spirit must have taken your form and came home to live with us. That's why they never returned to the inn for you when you fell sick.

GRANDMOTHER:

So then you have known me all your life, in the shape of that demon?

TRIPITAKA:

Yes, yes. And I loved you very much.

GRANDMOTHER:

And you are happy?

TRIPITAKA:

Yes. I am.

GRANDMOTHER:

Then I am happy too. Grandson, I am very ill, but if you kiss my eyes I do believe that I may see you once.

[TRIPITAKA *complies. His* GRANDMOTHER *sees him and dies in his arms. The* DEATH GIRLS *enter with their warrant and black cloth.*]

TRIPITAKA:

No. No. Not yet.

[*The* DEATH GIRLS *gently take* GRANDMOTHER *from his arms, roll her in the cloth, and drag her off.*]

SHA MONK:

Master, you must know that when leaves are strong and green, no wind on Earth can shake them from the tree, for it is not their time. But when the leaves are dry and old, well, then they fall like rain. This is how it ever was with mortal creatures.

MONKEY:

Master, understand: this means that you are coming very close now to your origin.

WORDLESS SCRIPTURE

[*Music. The pilgrims journey briefly. The music ends.*]

TRIPITAKA:

Pilgrims, the landscape seems to be changing, but the other day those mendicant monks told us it was still two thousand miles to the kingdom of India. How far could we have come?

MONKEY:

Master, you always talk of distances in miles. Could it be that you have forgotten all your masters taught you in the monastery?

TRIPITAKA:

What are you saying? Is there a single day I don't recite the Buddhist sutras that I know? How can you say I have forgotten them?

MONKEY:

But when it comes to their true interpretation, you don't know a thing.

TRIPITAKA:

Ape head! How dare you say I don't know how to interpret scripture? Do you?

[MONKEY *stares at* TRIPITAKA *in silence.* TRIPITAKA *stares back. They do not move.*]

PIG:

What brassiness! Like me, he began his Buddhist career as a monster spirit. He was never even an acolyte, let alone a seminarian. Elder Brother, why are you silent now? Let's hear the lecture! Please, give us your interpretation!

SHA MONK:

Second Elder Brother, can you believe him? Pilgrim Sun is giving us a tall tale just to goad Master on his journey. He doesn't know anything about explaining a sutra!

TRIPITAKA:

Sha Monk, Bajie, stop your babbling! Pilgrim Sun's interpretation is made in silence. That is true interpretation.

JADE EMPEROR:

And in that moment of insight, our disciples, without noticing and without taking a step, slipped over the border into the realm of the West.

THE PRINCESS OF SRAVASTI

[*Music, an Indian raga. The* JADE EMPEROR *exits. The pilgrims gaze around.*]

TRIPITAKA:

Could this be the kingdom of Sravasti?

PIG:

This is quite strange, Master! I have followed you now for years, and I have never known you to recognize the way before. Today, you seem to know where you are.

TRIPITAKA:

It's not quite like that. It's just that in studying the sutras, I have read about the Jetavana Park in the city of Sravasti. This place resembles the description. In any case, this is a new territory, and we must have our travel rescript certified.

MONKEY:

Master, I will escort you to the king's court.

PIG:

I'll go too.

SHA MONK:

Second Elder Brother, you shouldn't. Your features are not the most attractive. What could you do when you arrived at the court gate?

TRIPITAKA:

Sha Monk is quite right. Our Idiot is too rough and coarse.

PIG:

Master, why are you abandoning me? There's not that much difference in the way the three of us look.

TRIPITAKA:
We're going, Bajie. Stay here with Sha Monk.

[PIG *and* SHA MONK *depart. Suddenly, a great many* VILLAGERS *appear, shouting and running around excitedly.*]

VILLAGERS [*severally*]:
It's time to toss the ball! Where's the princess? Is she coming? [*And so on.*]

[MONKEY *grabs a* VILLAGER.]

MONKEY:
Tell me, sir, is your king in court today? We are travelers who need our rescript certified.

VILLAGER:
You've picked an auspicious day. The king's daughter turns twenty today, and she is about to choose her husband.

MONKEY:
Oh?

VILLAGER:
We've built a tower for her in the middle of the city. She's going up there now, and she'll toss down a ball to determine which person she will take for her husband; the ball will land closest to the man she is destined for.

PRINCESS [*from above*]:
All right! Here goes!

TRIPITAKA:

Isn't it odd, pilgrim, how the people in this place all seem the same as those of the land back east? I am thinking now about my mother and how she met the man she was destined to marry. Isn't it strange that they should have this custom here also? Shall we head to court?

[*The* PRINCESS's *ball lands squarely on* TRIPITAKA's *head.*]

VILLAGER:
It hit a priest!

[*Enormous jubilation. Confetti, dancing, wedding music.*]

TRIPITAKA [*frantic*]:
What do I do now?

MONKEY [*laughing*]:
Relax, Master!

TRIPITAKA:
How can you be laughing at a time like this?

[PIG *and* SHA MONK *arrive.*]

SHA MONK:
What's going on?

MONKEY:
Master's found true happiness!

TRIPITAKA:

Will you shut up! Get me out of this!

[*The* PRINCESS *and her* FATHER, *the* KING, *approach.*]

PRINCESS:

Oh, he's so handsome! We must have met in a past life!

FATHER KING:

Are you happy, then?

PRINCESS [*to* TRIPITAKA]:

You are the one I wish to marry.

TRIPITAKA:

Release me and pardon me! I am a scripture pilgrim!

PIG [*to* SHA MONK]:

I knew I should have gone with him! If it hadn't been for you the ball would have struck me, and the princess would have had to take me in! That would have been marvelous! What an arrangement! We'd play and play!

SHA MONK:

If that ball had struck you, a letter of annulment sent overnight wouldn't be fast enough. You think they'd take a catastrophe like you inside the door?

FATHER KING:

This monk is most unreasonable! If he persists in refusing, have the embroidered-uniformed guards push him out and execute him.

TRIPITAKA:

This was my father's destiny, but I am not my father! Pilgrim!

MONKEY [*still laughing*]:

Master, what can I do?

[*Suddenly* GUANYIN *appears. All of the* VILLAGERS *drop to the ground, unconscious.*]

GUANYIN:

Why do you keep me waiting such a long time, Tripitaka? It's been nearly sixteen years since you set out, and still you are anxious and restless and you delay yourself over and over.

TRIPITAKA:

Forgive me, Lady Bodhisattva, but—have you killed them? Are they alive or dead?

GUANYIN:

Alive but lost in a dream, as always. But you, my scripture pilgrim, you must wake up. You have slept long enough.

MONKEY:

Quick, get the rescript certified.

[PIG *gets the rescript and ink from the basket and stamps the rescript with the hand of the unconscious* FATHER KING.]

GUANYIN:

Look to your origin, Tripitaka Tang.

[*She departs. The* VILLAGERS *begin to stir.*]

MONKEY:
Hurry, before these people wake, let's go!

REUNION ON THE RIVER

[*Music. The pilgrims run off; the* VILLAGERS *awake and disperse. The* JADE EMPEROR *enters.*]

JADE EMPEROR:
Now, at last, our four pilgrims, walking in step and thinking as one, could see in the distance the great Thunderclap Mountain of the Western Heaven, floating halfway up in the air surrounded by a pure gold light. The surpassing scenery all around is saturated with flowers and grass, pine and bamboo, phoenix, cranes, and deer. Here, on the very brink of Heaven, there lies a final river some eight or nine miles wide. Our pilgrims find themselves upon its only bridge, which ends abruptly in midair.

[*The pilgrims are high on the bridge. The* JADE EMPEROR *exits.*]

TRIPITAKA:
Pilgrim Sun, clearly this bridge is not for human beings to cross. There must be some other way.

MONKEY:
This is the way! This is the way!

PIG:
If this is the way, who dares to cross? I can't see the beginning or the ending of this bridge!

MONKEY:
Come on, it's not so bad!

PIG:
It's too difficult! Too difficult!

MONKEY:
If you don't cross this bridge, you'll never gain redemption! You'll never be a Buddha!

[GUANYIN *enters below, pulling behind her, by a long string, a little boat with a tiny lantern.*]

PIG:
I don't care!

TRIPITAKA:
Disciples, stop this frivolity! I see something coming this way. Is it a boat, floating to the shore?

MONKEY:
Master is right! A boat is coming for us!

TRIPITAKA:
But no one is guiding it—

MONKEY:
Never mind, Master, it is for us. Come on!

[*The pilgrims exit.* GUANYIN *continues slowly until she disappears. Music continues as the river materializes onstage. The pilgrims reenter, riding on a large version of the boat with its lantern. A figure, dressed identically to* TRIPITAKA, *is rolling on the water.*]

TRIPITAKA:
Disciples, I see something in the water.

SHA MONK:
Be careful, Master, don't lean out so far!

TRIPITAKA:
Can't you see? There's something over there! I must find out what it is.

SHA MONK:
Please! Sit down, Master!

TRIPITAKA:
No—

MONKEY:
Let him go—

TRIPITAKA:
I must see what it is—

PIG:
Master, what are you doing—

SHA MONK:
Sit down, Master, you can't even swim! You'll sink to the bottom!

MONKEY:
Let him go!

[TRIPITAKA *slowly steps out of the boat and begins to walk on the surface of the water toward the figure. The music is one long, sustained note.*]

SHA MONK:
Master is walking on the water.

[TRIPITAKA *reaches the figure, kneels down, and looks into his face.*]

MONKEY:
What is it, Master? What have you found?

TRIPITAKA:
Disciples, it is myself.

MONKEY:
Congratulations! You have transcended!

PIG:
Congratulations, Master!

[TRIPITAKA *holds the figure in his arms. The music shifts to the raga Jog, the raga of unification.*]

SHA MONK:
Congratulations. It's you, Master!

MONKEY:
Let him float away, Master. Go on. Let him float away.

[TRIPITAKA *releases the figure, and it floats away. Then he picks up a rope attached to the boat, and as* GUANYIN *pulled the little boat, he pulls the large boat off as the music rises. As the pilgrims disappear, the entire heavenly court comes forward:* GUANYIN, *the* JADE EMPEROR, SUBODHI, MOKSA, *and all the other heavenly* IMMORTALS. *After they are formally arranged, the pilgrims enter.* TRIPITAKA *is wearing the scarlet robe and a scarlet hat. The other pilgrims have ceremonial hats as well. After they have entered,* BUDDHA *enters. The music that has played continuously since the pilgrims' departure from the city of Sravasti ends.*]

THE WESTERN HEAVEN

MOKSA [*announcing*]:
The pilgrims Tripitaka Tang, Sun Wukong, Zhu Wuneng, and Sha Wujing.

BUDDHA:
May I see your travel rescript?

[PIG *hands it to* MOKSA, *who hands it to* BUDDHA. *It is by now a pathetic, shredded, dirty scrap.*]

TRIPITAKA:
By the decree of the Tang Emperor in the land of the East, your disciple has come to beg you for the true scriptures for the redemption of humanity. I implore Buddha Tathagata to vouchsafe his grace and grant my wish.

BUDDHA:
What has been the disposition of the four pilgrims during their journey?

GUANYIN:

They showed genuine devotion and determination.

BUDDHA:

In your land of the East there is a great deal of greed and killing, oppression, and deceit. I have baskets of scriptures that can deliver humanity from its afflictions and dispel its calamities. Since you have come such a great distance, I would give you all of them, but the people of your region would only mock the true words. Therefore, I grant you three rolls of scripture. Moksa, fetch the three rolls from our treasure loft—those that treat most particularly the quest for origin—and give them to our pilgrims as a token of our grace.

[MOKSA *goes to fetch the rolls of scripture.* ATTENDANTS *come forward with bowls for* PIG *and* SHA MONK.]

I have prepared a special meal for you. This time, it is you, Bajie, and you, Sha Monk, who are in luck, for this meal will dissolve the last of your mortal substance and return your immortal nature. Through the merit you have gained by aiding this monk, you are redeemed.

[MOKSA *hands the scriptures to* TRIPITAKA.]

The efficacy of these scriptures cannot be measured. Honor them and treasure them.

[*Everyone bows.*]

I have asked the Vajra Guardians to carry you back to the land of the East. Farewell, Tripitaka Tang.

THE EIGHTY-FIRST ORDEAL

[*Music. The court disperses except for four* IMMORTALS *who step forward. The pilgrims ride on their backs.* GUANYIN *reenters with* MOKSA, *above.*]

GUANYIN:
Moksa, read to me again the account of the master's ordeals.

MOKSA [*unrolling a scroll*]:
Being almost killed at birth is the first ordeal. Being thrown in a river hardly a month old is the second ordeal.

GUANYIN:
Skip ahead.

MOKSA:
Confronting the Robbers of Six Senses is the fifteenth ordeal. Bringing the Mind Monkey to submission is the sixteenth ordeal.

GUANYIN:
Skip ahead.

MOKSA:
Bringing the body of Bajie to submission is the twentieth ordeal. Hard to Cross Eight Hundred Mile Wide River is the twenty-first ordeal.

GUANYIN:
Go to the end, the end.

MOKSA:

Being almost married to a princess is the seventy-ninth ordeal.
Crossing the Cloud-Transcending River is the eightieth ordeal.

[MOKSA *rolls up the scroll.*]

GUANYIN:

Eightieth ordeal? Eightieth?

[*She grabs the scroll and searches through it, increasingly frantic.*]

Buddha decreed there should be eighty-one ordeals! Nine times
nine is the perfect number! One ordeal is missing. [*Shouting to the*
VAJRA GUARDIANS] Drop them!

MOKSA:

But Lady Bodhisattva, they are five hundred miles up in the air!

GUANYIN:

Drop them!

[*Music stops. The* VAJRA GUARDIANS *dump the pilgrims off their
backs and exit. The four pilgrims lie on the ground waving their
arms and legs in the air and screaming as though falling from a
great height. Then with a loud bang of arms and legs, they "land."*]

PIG:

Where are we? What happened?

MONKEY:

Those devilish immortals dropped us!

PIG:

I thought only profane people would practice this sort of fraud. Buddha commanded them to take us back east and they drop us in midair!

MONKEY:

Stop grumbling!

[TRIPITAKA *has his face covered with his hands and is shaking.*]

SHA MONK:

Something is wrong with the Tang monk.

MONKEY:

Oh no! Master, don't cry! How can you behave like this after the journey you have made? Master, please!

[TRIPITAKA *uncovers his face; he is laughing.*]

TRIPITAKA:

I'm not crying ... What an excellent joke the Buddha has played on us! Just when—just when we thought—we thought we were free and clear ... to send us this last ordeal ...!

MONKEY [*starting to laugh*]:

It's true ... we were flying along and they just dropped us!

[PIG *imitates all of them falling and shouting like idiots. Everyone laughs.*]

SHA MONK [*laughing*]:
We thought we were done, and now . . . there's still ten thousand miles to go!

PIG:
And just as many rivers!

TRIPITAKA [*pretending to sober up*]:
No, really, disciples, this is a very serious matter.

[*He laughs. They all join in.*]

GUANYIN [*above*]:
The eighty-first ordeal: falling from the sky in the middle of your life, losing all your labor and in response? Laughing. They have passed the final trial. Nothing can ever harm them again.

[GUANYIN *and* MOKSA *depart.*]

TRIPITAKA [*serious at last*]:
So where do you suppose we are?

MONKEY:
How should I know?

[MONKEY *cracks up. They all do. Some* VILLAGERS *approach.*]

FIRST VILLAGER:
Look, there they are, like I told you—four immortals fallen from the sky!

SECOND VILLAGER:

Quick! We must alert the entire village and bring them out.

FIRST VILLAGER:

Immortals! You have blessed us with this fall. Please stay here for a while and enjoy our hospitality!

[*The* VILLAGERS *dart off. Music.*]

MONKEY:

Master, quickly, we must fly! This town will keep us here feasting I don't know how long!

PIG:

How can we escape? They are already coming down the hill!

MONKEY:

Master, do you see that bird flying overhead?

SHA MONK:

Master, there isn't any choice.

MONKEY:

It's as simple as that, Master.

PIG:

Come on! There's no more time—

SHA MONK:

They're coming, Master, we'll be stuck here for days!

PIG:

They're bound to force their food on us and . . . and I don't feel the slightest bit hungry!

MONKEY:

Are you ready, Master?

SHA MONK:

Don't think.

MONKEY:

Don't think, Master. Look at the little bird.

PIG:

Let's go! Now!

[*The music rises. The four pilgrims step forward slowly, and then* TRIPITAKA *begins to fly. They all fly off. Members of the* TANG COURT *appear holding pine tree branches that slowly tilt and point toward the east.* GUANYIN *crosses the stage on a white cloud of silk. The* TANG EMPEROR *enters with the rest of the* TANG COURT. *He is older now, wears spectacles, and leans on a cane. The white silk is turned over and becomes a little blue stream.* TRIPITAKA, MONKEY, PIG, *and* SHA MONK *enter. The latter three sit down humbly. With great ease,* TRIPITAKA *steps over the final, narrow river. Music ends.*]

WILD-GOOSE PAGODA TEMPLE AND CONCLUSION

TANG EMPEROR:

Has our bond brother returned?

TRIPITAKA:
My emperor, he has.

TANG EMPEROR:
Who are these three persons?

TRIPITAKA:
They are my disciples.

TANG EMPEROR [*puzzled by their appearance*]:
Are your noble disciples . . . foreigners?

TRIPITAKA:
My humble disciples were living as monsters deep in the wilds. Due to past crimes against Heaven, each was in need of redemption. Thanks to the admonitions of the Bodhisattva Guanyin, each one was converted and helped me along the way. Through this act they have gained merit and are once again immortal. Sun Wukong, Zhu Wuneng, and Sha Wujing, I thank you.

[*He bows to his disciples.*]

MONKEY:
Between us, Master, there can be no word of thanks, for each of us is equally indebted to the other. We are meant to support one another; and from the merit of each we have each found our liberation.

TANG EMPEROR:
How quietly and how courteously your disciples bear themselves. May I see your travel rescript?

[TRIPITAKA *hands him the little scrap. The* TANG EMPEROR *looks at it politely.*]

And the scriptures, did you retrieve them?

TRIPITAKA:
Your subject has brought his emperor three scrolls containing 5,048 scriptures.

TANG EMPEROR:
Tomorrow morning we will meet at the Wild-Goose Pagoda Temple to formally honor you and welcome you home.

[*Everyone bows and begins to leave.*]

Tripitaka, my bond brother, tell me, what is it like?

TRIPITAKA:
Your Majesty?

TANG EMPEROR:
The world. What is it like?

[MUSIC. *The two join arms and walk,* TRIPITAKA *speaking and the* TANG EMPEROR *listening. The day passes, then the night, and now it is morning at the Wild-Goose Pagoda Temple. Everyone reassembles.*]

We did not sleep the whole night when we reflected on how great and profound has been the merit of our brother, such that no compensation is quite adequate. Finally, we composed in our head a few homely sentences as a mere token of our gratitude. Let us recite our composition for you:

We so love our Heaven and Earth that we forever strive to make and gaze upon their image. We make and remake the world, populating it with pictures of itself into which we gaze in hope of both losing and then finding our true selves. We are drawn to these images with a longing that is the longing for our own origin.

But the force that animates or moves or causes change has no image. It is invisible. We know the seasons by the shifting fields of color, but what makes the seasons change? Why does life hold us, then let us go?

And if it is difficult to understand the true nature of the world given only these elusive and fleeting images, how much more difficult it is to understand the nature of Buddhism, which holds to silence, darkness, and stillness; for it is within these things—emptiness, formlessness, and silence—that the divine resides.

[*The* TANG EMPEROR *stops speaking. There is total silence and stillness for half a minute or so.*]

Let us recite:

[*Music, a sustained tone. As* ALL *recite, they slowly leave.*]

ALL:
I submit to the Buddha of the Past, Present, and Future
I submit to the Buddha of Pure Joy
I submit to the Buddha Amitabha
I submit to the Buddha of Sky and Water
I submit—

[*Everyone but* GUANYIN *and* TRIPITAKA *stops moving in midstep.* GUANYIN *whispers.*]

GUANYIN:
Tripitaka! Tripitaka Tang.

TRIPITAKA:
Bodhisattva?

GUANYIN:
Come with me.

TRIPITAKA:
Where?

GUANYIN:
To the Western Heaven.

TRIPITAKA:
Why?

GUANYIN:
To live.

TRIPITAKA:
For how long?

GUANYIN:
Forever.

[GUANYIN *takes* TRIPITAKA *by the hand. Everyone begins to move and recite again as these two move toward Heaven.*]

ALL:
I submit to the Buddha, Light of the Sun and Moon
I submit to the Buddha of Wondrous Tone and Sound
I submit to the Buddha, Lamp That Scans the World
I submit to the Buddha Tripitaka Tang
I submit to the Bodhisattva Guanyin
I submit

[*Everyone is still but* SHA MONK *and* PIG.]

SHA MONK:
What shall you do, Brother, now that our journey is at an end? We
stand at the threshold of Heaven. Shall we enter?

PIG:
Brother, I have acquired a taste for travel, and I think that I should
like to continue. As Buddha has said to his monks: Walk over the
Earth for the blessing of many, for the happiness of many; walk over
the Earth out of compassion for the world, for the welfare and the
blessing and the happiness of gods and men.

SHA MONK:
Brother, may I join you?

[*They bow to each other, join arms, and start to go.*]

ALL:
I submit to the Bodhisattva Sun Wukong
I submit to the Bodhisattva Zhu Wuneng
I submit to the Bodhisattva Sha Wujing

[*Everyone is still but the* TANG EMPEROR *and* MONKEY. *The* TANG EMPEROR *hands a scripture scroll to* MONKEY *and addresses the audience.*]

TANG EMPEROR:
We wish to use these words
To adorn Buddha's pure land—
To repay fourfold grace above
And save those on the path below.
If there are those who see and hear,
Their minds will find enlightenment.
Their births with us in paradise
Will be this body's recompense.

[MONKEY *unrolls the scroll and begins to read.*]

MONKEY:
One hundred two thousand six hundred years ago, the Heaven and the Earth made love, and everything was born.

TANG EMPEROR:
Here ends the journey to the West.

A NOTE ON CASTING

In the original production of *Journey to the West*, there were fourteen actors (five women and nine men) and three musicians, but the play would be easier to do with an even larger cast. The original division of roles appears below, with roles listed in approximate order of appearance, but role assignments could easily break down in other ways. From scene to scene, the number of heavenly immortals, villagers, monkeys, courtiers, and so on, needn't be consistent.

FIRST WOMAN: Guanyin, Girl ("Hearts of Desire"), Spider Woman and Cave Bear ("Parade of Demons")

SECOND WOMAN: Buddha, Daoist Disciple, Dragon Queen, Death Girl, Peach Girl, Woodsman Li, Apricot, Spider Woman ("Parade of Demons"), Villager

THIRD WOMAN: A Monkey, Daoist Disciple, Death Girl, Peach Girl, Green Orchid, Ferrywoman, Spider Woman and White Bone Demon ("Parade of Demons")

FOURTH WOMAN: A Monkey, Subodhi, Buddhist in the Tang Court, Robber, Grandmother, Innkeeper, Spider Woman ("Parade of Demons")

FIFTH WOMAN: A Monkey, Daoist Disciple, Death Girl, Peach Girl, Buddhist in the Tang Court, Tripitaka's Mother, Fisherman Zhang, Princess of Sravasti, Moon's Mistress

FIRST MAN: Jade Emperor, Tang Emperor, Tripitaka's Father, Daoist Guardian, King ("Hearts of Desire")

SECOND MAN: Monkey King

THIRD MAN: First Monkey, Dragon King Attendant, Robber, Pig

FOURTH MAN: Moksa, Daoist Disciple, Dragon King Attendant, Robber, Master Void-Surmounting, Villager

FIFTH MAN: Second Monkey, Immortal, Tripitaka

SIXTH MAN: Third Monkey, Robber, Sha Monk

SEVENTH MAN: A Monkey, Woodcutter, Immortal, Robber, Boatman, Cloud-Brushing Dean, Daoist Father-in-Law, Yellow Fiend ("Parade of Demons")

EIGHTH MAN: A Monkey, Fiend, Yama, Robber, Lonesome Rectitude, Ghost King ("Parade of Demons"), Monk ("Hearts of Desire"), Father King ("The Princess of Sravasti")

NINTH MAN: A Monkey, Dragon King, Mr. Gao, Eight-and-Ten, Officer ("Hearts of Desire"), Villager

MUSICIANS AND THEIR INSTRUMENTS

FIRST MUSICIAN: Thai harp

SECOND MUSICIAN: brass tubular bells; Chinese bass drum; Balinese suling (bamboo flute); soparinino recorder; Persian nay (endblown flute); Tibetan dramnyan (long-neck lute); Indian pakhawaj (double-headed drum); Thai angklung (bamboo shakers); Tibetan monastic cymbals; vichitra vina; North Indian sarod and tabla; various other small percussion instruments, horns, and bells

THIRD MUSICIAN: violin

APPENDIX: ADDITIONAL NOTES ON THE STAGING OF *JOURNEY TO THE WEST*

Reading the script might lead anyone seriously considering directing or producing the play to think it is full of impossible, or impossibly expensive, effects. This isn't the case. A simple, rough-and-tumble production would serve the story very well. Below are some of the tricks used in the original production.

SCENE SHIFTS

Each scene should step right on the heel of the previous one. The narration of the Jade Emperor and Guanyin takes us from one place to another instantly. This narration should be fairly transparent—that is to say it should always draw attention to the scene and not the speaker. So while inflected with character, its primary function is not revelation of character but revelation of action and scene.

RIVERS, STREAMS, AND OCEANS

Most bodies of water were made with silk manipulated into little waves by members of the company. At the end of "The Eighty-first Ordeal," Guanyin crossed the stage just upstage of a length of white silk made to ripple and float like clouds. This cloth was then turned over, revealing a deep-blue side, and became the final three-foot river that Tripitaka easily steps over as he is greeted by the Tang Emperor. The river on which Tripitaka finds his own body was made by members of the company sitting around the stage holding and manipulating blue fans.

MONKEY'S MOUNTAIN, BOAT, AND
GOLDEN-HOOPED ROD

When he is banished from Heaven and sentenced to five hundred years of punishment, Monkey was put under a miniature mountain placed over an open trap. The mountain had a little window for his eye to show through. However, when Tripitaka climbs the mountain to pull the tab and free Monkey, he climbed up the stairs to a little mountain set in the back-wall opening. Many times the staging resorted to similar shifts in scale.

Monkey's first boat was a wok. He sat inside and rocked it back and forth by the handles. It could also be a basket. As he made his first ocean journey, Guanyin held a tiny replica of the wok in her hand and dropped blue confetti on it for rain, while at the same time larger blue bits of paper floated down from the proscenium on the real, life-sized Monkey.

One of the tricks of the show was how Monkey's little rod became full-size. The performer would take the three-inch rod from behind his ear and pretend to throw it to the ground with an emphatic gesture while actually palming it. The stage had a few strategically placed small holes in its surface through which a full-size rod would come shooting up, propelled manually by crew members through a little chute under the floor. All of this was always accompanied by a loud cymbal crash. If your stage has no large trap area below, I'd just have Monkey toss the little rod offstage and someone toss back the big one; or perhaps pretend to throw the little rod straight up and have the big one drop down from on high; or have Guanyin simply hand him the full-size rod.

FLYING

Flying was a "let's pretend" affair. It can be done in any of the numerous ways a child would invent. In our case, the performers, moving slowly, did as follows: Step on one foot, bend forward from the waist while drawing arms across the chest. Then simultaneously unfold and extend arms out to the side while rising on one leg and extending the other behind, so that the body is balanced on one leg perpendicular to the stage, arms extended. Then, still mostly bent over, step forward on the leg that had been extended behind, fold up the arms. Repeat.

One exception to this method of flying was in "The Tang Court" scene in act 1. When Guanyin came disguised to court to seek out and examine Tripitaka, she was temporarily played by a male performer. At the moment of her revelation, the male performer crumpled to the floor, and the "actual" Guanyin was flown in from above on a simple dropped line.

In Heaven, a few immortals were represented as floating by wearing little platforms around their waists on which were built fake pillows topped with fake, seated, crossed legs. The little platforms were initially draped to the floor in fabric painted like a sky with clouds. Later we discovered that simple black material made the illusion stronger.

Flying birds were present in the entr'acte and when Tripitaka learns to fly. In all cases the birds were actors pretending to be birds, but they could be little puppets or shadows.

There was one more very beautiful flying trick. When Tripitaka follows the bird and finally learns to fly, the villagers appeared climbing up metal ladder rungs embedded in the back wall. The villagers hooked their legs up to the knee in these rungs, braced their feet against the wall, and then leaned backward into the playing space so that their bodies were perpendicular to the floor. Tilting their faces up and looking straight out and upside-down toward the audience, they removed their hats and waved. It was as though the theater had pivoted ninety degrees—the audience had the illusion of being in the sky looking down at the villagers while simultaneously watching the pilgrims fly head-on.

Even if your theater is equipped for everyone to fly all over the place on wires, I still caution against that route. I'm afraid it would just slow things down and privilege too much technological trickery over cooperatively manufactured illusion.

HAVOC IN HEAVEN

The ferocious battle in Heaven where Monkey goes nuts over being a stable boy was done in slow motion, which made it easier for the audience to observe several near-simultaneous actions. In addition to all the fighting and immortals being knocked around, the audience could also witness Bajie (Pig) make a pass at the moon's mistress and Sha Monk trip and drop the jade vase. Sha Monk carried a vase on a pillow. The vase was attached on its upstage side to a long pole discreetly held by a performer upstage of Sha Monk. When Sha Monk tripped, the vase could go flying and whirling up and crash below the upstage lip of the playing area. Sha Monk could then reach down below the lip and retrieve a large piece of broken vase.

MUSIC

The musicians were visible onstage, residing in a roughly eight-foot-wide alley between the main playing space and the back wall where there was room enough for their instruments. This alley was at stage level, about eighteen inches below the main playing deck, and was also useful for little illusions such as the infant Tripitaka floating away in a basket of reeds, the villagers skating across the ice in "Eight Hundred Mile Wide River and Tripitaka's Story," and the illusion of the broken vase mentioned above.

Music was in every scene and helped accomplish every shift of scene. Sometimes it was discreetly enriched with recorded tracks, as in the long cue leading the pilgrims across the final river and into the Western Heaven. It accompanied almost every narrative passage, and it supported the action and sometimes commented on it ironically, as when the violinist came forward to stand behind Pig and play a sort of "sob story" melody as he told his life story. All this said, recorded music would serve, but I encourage original music for every production.

COSTUMES

Because they were so numerous and had to be changed so quickly, costumes were rather basic. Each of the ensemble members had a unique outfit—usually some sort of tunic and pants—to which he or she added various pieces, for example long red gloves with long hanging sleeves sewn on served to create elegant ladies. Various vests, jackets, and very simple robes created different looks for villagers, courtiers, Daoists, attendants, and so on. The monkeys all had belts with bouncy tails that curled up at the end. Only Guanyin and the Jade and Tang emperors had very elaborate costumes. In order to emphasize that the end of the journey and the origin of the journey are actually the same point, the Jade and Tang emperors were played by the same actor, and the two costumes were identical save that one was green and the other yellow. The Buddha had a train on his robe that was twenty-five feet long. All of his entrances were from the upper doors in the back wall. As he progressed down the stairs, his saffron train slithered down behind him like a slow waterfall. Various kinds of hats—Daoist-disciple hats, a wedding hat for the Princess, elaborate headgear for the emperors—added a great deal. With a cast of fourteen, there are dozens of quick costume changes. One actor alone had twenty-four.

POSSIBLE CUTS

The show is long. Quite long. There are several possible and easy cuts you could make that wouldn't pain you as they would have me. The scene with the Woodcutter may be cut by altering the Jade Emperor's introductory line to: "Monkey searched a long time until he came upon a tall and beautiful mountain with thick forests at its base. He went straight to the top to look around. Imagine his delight when he saw, approaching from a distance, what looked to be a cloud floating a few feet above the Earth." And here bring on the Daoists. You could cut the second tea-drinking scene with the Dragon King where Monkey asks about the painting and simply have Guanyin come upon Monkey on the road. The entr'acte at the top of act 2 could be left out. Another option is to remove Apricot's appearance in "The Brambles of Philosophy" and have the other pilgrims interrupt the scene earlier. Finally, you could cut an entire adventure in the second act—either "The Women of Western Liang," "The Brambles of Philosophy," or "Hearts of Desire."

THREE FINAL SUGGESTIONS

First, don't do the play unless you have someone in mind who can play Monkey. He (or she) must be a superb comic actor, witty, and both physically and mentally agile. He must have enormous stamina and great charm. My own Doug Hara had all of this as well as the ability to do standing backflips and other simian moves. Yet if you are faced with a difficult choice, go with the smarter, funnier actor rather than the more physically skilled actor. Monkey is agile and tricky physically only because he is an embodiment of the mind; it is the quick, flexible mind itself that is most important in the actor.

Second, resist the temptation to lard your production's program and preproduction literature with too much somber and learned information about Buddhism and Daoism and so on. A little is enough. Don't make the audience study up in order to see the show. It will frighten them and give them far too respectful an attitude toward the play. If the audience is primed with too much serious-minded, earnest dramaturgical information in advance, they are confused, even offended, when the curtain comes up and the stage is almost immediately occupied by a bunch of screeching monkeys, and it will be well into the first act before they shift their attitude and begin to enjoy themselves. The play—the story—has a simple, adventurous, and comic surface, and the discourse surrounding the production should mirror its unpretentious nature.

Finally, there was no attempt in the conception or staging of our production to mimic Chinese opera or any other classical Chinese theatrical form. The adaptation was not written with that form in mind, and neither the language nor the structure of the play supports such an approach. It was intended to be only what it can be: a Western iteration of one of the great works of global literature.

ABOUT THE PLAYWRIGHT

Mary Zimmerman's credits as an adapter and a director include *Metamorphoses, The Arabian Nights, The Odyssey, Argonautika, Eleven Rooms of Proust, Silk, The Secret in the Wings, Mirror of the Invisible World,* and *The Notebooks of Leonardo da Vinci.* Her work has been produced at the Lookingglass Theatre and Goodman Theatre of Chicago; on Broadway at Circle in the Square; in New York at Second Stage, the Brooklyn Academy of Music, and the Manhattan Theatre Club; at the Mark Taper Forum in Los Angeles; and at the McCarter, Berkeley Repertory, and Seattle Repertory, as well as many other theaters around the country and abroad. The recipient of a Tony Award for directing for *Metamorphoses* and a MacArthur Fellowship, Zimmerman is a professor of performance studies at Northwestern University.

Monkey (Doug Hara) and the Woodcutter (Kelvin Han Yee)

Monkey (Doug Hara) weighs a weapon at the home of the Dragon King (Tim Rhoze).

Subhodi (Lisa Tejero) flanked by two other heavenly immortals (Bruce Norris and Marc Vann), with the Dragon King (Tim Rhoze) and Yama (David Kersnar); Guanyin (Jenny Bacon) and the Jade Emperor (Christopher Donahue) look on from the bridge.

Buddha (Jane Cho) and Monkey (Doug Hara)

Monkey (Doug Hara) meets Tripitaka (Bruce Norris).

Tripitaka (Nelson Mashita) and Monkey (Doug Hara) at the house of Mr. Gao (Kelvin Han Yee)

The pilgrims, led by a bird, begin to fly ("The Eighty-first Ordeal").

Tripitaka (Bruce Norris) ascends, guided by Guanyin (Jenny Bacon), at the conclusion of the play; Tang Emperor (Chris Donahue) in foreground